The Triumph of Profiling

The Triumph of Profiling

The Self in Digital Culture

Andreas Bernard

Translated by Valentine A. Pakis

polity

First published in German as *Komplizen des Erkennungsdienstes. Das Selbst in der digitalen Kultur*

Polity Press
65 Bridge Street
Cambridge CB2 1UR, UK

Polity Press
101 Station Landing
Suite 300
Medford, MA 02155, USA

ISBN-13: 978-1-5095-3629-0
ISBN-13: 978-1-5095-3630-6 (pb)

A catalogue record for this book is available from the British Library.

Library of Congress Cataloging-in-Publication Data

Names: Bernard, Andreas, 1969- author.
Title: The triumph of profiling : the self in digital culture / Andreas Bernard.
Other titles: Komplizen des Erkennungsdienstes. English
Description: Cambridge : Polity Press, 2019. | Translation of: Komplizen des Erkennungsdienstes. | Includes bibliographical references and index.
Identifiers: LCCN 2018050589 (print) | LCCN 2018051482 (ebook) | ISBN 9781509536313 (Epub) | ISBN 9781509536290 (hardback) | ISBN 9781509536306 (pbk.)
Subjects: LCSH: Self-presentation–Social aspects. | Self-perception–Social aspects. | Social representations. | Personality assessment. | Social media–Psychological aspects. | Subjectivity.
Classification: LCC HM1066 (ebook) | LCC HM1066 .B4713 2019 (print) | DDC 126–dc23
LC record available at https://lccn.loc.gov/2018050589

Typeset in 10.5 on 12 pt Sabon Roman by Toppan Best-set Premedia Limited
Printed and bound in the UK by CPI Group (UK) Ltd, Croydon

For further information on Polity, visit our website: politybooks.com

Contents

1
Profiles: The Development of a Format

An old political debate reopened when, within just a few months in 2012, the United States was shocked by two mass shootings, one in a movie theatre in Denver and the other at an elementary school in Connecticut. The question was whether there might be better ways to identify potential perpetrators in advance so as to prevent similar atrocities from happening in the future. To the familiar suspicious signs – the introverted nature of the predominantly male offenders, their social isolation, and their history of psychiatric treatment – was now added an additional criterion: the reluctance of the killers to participate on social media. As reporters were quick to point out, neither James Eagan Holmes nor Adam Lanza had a profile on Facebook, Twitter, or LinkedIn. Like the Norwegian Anders Breivik, who had committed a similar crime the year before, Holmes and Lanza refused to join the internet's omnipresent portals for communication and self-representation, and this refusal was being characterized as a warning sign. Recruitment managers at large companies reminded the public that it was now a common practice to look at the online profiles of job applicants and that an applicant's complete absence from social networks was highly peculiar. This opinion found support in a 2011 study conducted by the Canadian psychiatrist Richard Bélanger, who discovered a "u-shaped association" between internet activity and the mental health of adolescents: "Health care providers should thus be alerted both when caring for adolescents who do not use the Internet or use it rarely, as well as for those who are online several hours daily."[1] In today's digital culture, as this discussion makes clear, it is now a matter of irritation when people of a certain age have neglected to create a public double of themselves online in the form of profiles, status updates, comments, and so on. In the Western world, this abstinence has even become the first indication of psychiatric abnormality, perhaps of a mental illness or possibly of a latent pathological impulse that might one day be discharged in a harrowing act of violence. Conversely, the regular use of social media is now regarded as evidence of good health and normality.

My reflections in this book about the status of the self in digital culture are concerned with the methods, services, and devices that have become ubiquitous and, in light of their daily use, have increasingly come to seem like a natural disposition. In the history of the representation of subjectivity, however, they are in fact an astonishingly recent development. Anyone who attended school or university just a quarter-century ago will remember how few options were available then for representing one's own personality, preferences, and convictions to the public – a patch on the back of a jacket, a few lines beneath one's yearbook picture, or an expensive personal ad that would run for just one day in the local newspaper. This minimal radius of publicity for anyone without constant access to the mass media was still the invariable reality at the beginning of the 1990s, and yet those years now feel like a distant and unfamiliar epoch.

In no time at all – Facebook became open to everyone in the fall of 2006, and there have been smartphones since 2007 and app stores since 2008 – a comprehensive digital culture has emerged whose manifestations have been studied, celebrated, or demonized by journalists and academics on an ongoing basis. The origins of this culture in the history of knowledge, however, have seldom been discussed (and when they have been, it has been from the perspective of computer science). The aim of this book is to trace back just such a genealogy in order to demonstrate how digital media technologies have been embedded in the history of the human sciences. Ultimately, what is most striking about today's methods of self-representation and self-perception – the profiles of social media, but also the various locational functions on smartphones or the bodily measurements of the "quantified-self movement" – is the fact that they all derive from methods of criminology, psychology, or psychiatry that were conceived at various points since the end of the nineteenth century. Certain techniques for collecting data, which were long used exclusively by police detectives or scientific authorities to identify suspicious groups of people, are now being applied to everyone who uses a smartphone or social media. Biographical descriptions, GPS transmitters, and measuring devices installed on bodies are no longer just instruments for tracking suspected criminals but are now being used for the sake of having fun, communicating, making money, or finding a romantic partner.

A conceptual history of the profile in the twentieth century

In this regard, the category of the profile is especially instructive. As is well known, this element plays an essential role in any exchange conducted on social media. The profile of members on LinkedIn, Instagram, or Facebook – the place where they describe themselves and where their personal information, texts, photos, and videos are gathered – is the nodal point of interaction. Thus, even the earliest research devoted to social media placed the profile at the heart of its analysis. In her influential essays about Friendster, for instance, Danah Boyd repeatedly takes this element as her starting point. One of her pieces from 2006, co-written with Jeffrey Heer, begins as follows: "Profiles have become a common mechanism for presenting one's identity online."[2] To the creators of a profile, who are simultaneously its object, Boyd thus attributes a high degree of sovereignty. They enjoy complete autonomy in the public representation of their self, and the more original and comprehensive this representation is, the stronger the reaction it will entice from other users of the social network in question: "By paying the cost of carefully crafting an interesting profile," as Boyd and Judith Donath concluded about Friendster in 2004, "one can make more connections."[3] In her essays, Boyd frequently describes the practice of self-formation as an "identity performance," and she stresses that this creative and productive activity has "shifted the Profile from being a static representation of self to a communicative body in conversation with the other represented bodies."[4] This is therefore the great promise of the format: It is a free and self-determined space in which its creators can set the scene with a desirable, more or less honest, and more or less polished public persona.

Yet despite all of this, it should not be forgotten that, a mere 20 to 25 years ago, only serial killers and madmen were the objects of such profiles. Over the past quarter-century, this form of knowledge – this pattern for describing human beings – has experienced a rapid and profound transformation. In light of its use today, it would thus be informative to engage with the historical semantics of the concept. In which contexts and at which point in time did the written profile emerge? Who was its author, who was its object, and why was it created? In the sense of a "short, vivid biography outlining the most outstanding characteristics of the subject," as the 1968 edition of Webster's dictionary defines it,[5] the term has a relatively young history (German dictionaries and encyclopedias would not adopt this definition until later on). In the early modern era, the word "profile" was first used in architectural and geological contexts and denoted the contours of buildings or mountain ranges; in the eighteenth century, it also came to mean the side view of a face. It was apparently not until the early twentieth century that the profile was understood in the sense of a tabulated or schematic outline providing information about a person.

If my impression is correct, the word first appeared with this meaning as a technical term in the work of the Russian neurologist Grigory I. Rossolimo, who published an article in 1910 titled "Psychological Profiles." In this study, which was translated into German after the First World War and adopted by a number of psychologists, Rossolimo designed a procedure for measuring certain aptitudes among children – their attention span, memory capacity, associative ability, and so on – on a scale of one to ten. At the end of this testing procedure, according to Rossolimo, all of the "data points, which represented various levels of development, could be plotted on a diagram and connected to form a curve that would represent a detailed psychological profile" of the subject in question.[6] In Russia, these values were used above all to place children with behavioral problems into the appropriate types of schools. "The psychological profile," as Karl Bartsch noted in his adaptation of the method, "enables us to analyze and clarify the functions of the juvenile mind, and it reveals avenues toward the proper therapeutic and pedagogical treatment of diagnosed disorders."[7]

From the beginning, then, the epistemic interest of the profile consisted in providing evaluative information about the identity and behavior of deviant subjects. Bartsch, who refined the interpretation of Rossolimo's procedures and referred to his young patients as "psychopaths," asked the following about an ill-behaved child with a long history of behavioral problems: "Who can understand him without knowing his psychological profile?" He even calculated a precise relationship between a child's "profile curve" and how institutions should react to it: "All children from the age of 7 who do not achieve a profile score of 4," according to Bartsch's recommendation, "should be sent to a school for special education." What was always at stake whenever profiles were created – whenever, as the psychologist Fritz Giese wrote in 1923, "a sort of psychological cross-section could be drawn through human beings" – was the normality and healthiness of those being tested.[8]

Although the "psychological profile" in the sense outlined above went out of fashion around the year 1930, it soon reemerged in a new context of knowledge from where it would go on to gain widespread popularity in the late twentieth century. After the Second World War, concerted efforts were made in the United States to get to the bottom of unsolved crimes (especially those thought to have been committed by repeat offenders), and these efforts led to increased cooperation between criminologists and psychoanalysts. Just as conventional police work sought to analyze the material clues left at a crime scene in order to come closer to identifying the perpetrator, by means of fingerprints or bullet shells, the forensic-psychological perspective began to concentrate on immaterial and emotional clues – on the question, that is, of how such things as hatred, anger, rage, passion, or other eruptions of inner feelings might have left traces at the scene of a crime. Although this search for impressions left by the criminal personality – this practice of criminal-psychological ballistics – played a part in solving a number of spectacular serial crimes as early as the 1950s (for instance, the case of New York's "mad bomber," George Metesky), the method was first described as "psychiatric profiling" in a 1962 essay about notorious arsonists by the psychoanalyst Louis Gold.[9]

One major difference distinguished the "psychiatric profile" of criminology from the earlier use of the term in applied psychology: it was now the case that *unknown* persons were meant to be identified by means of this gathering of knowledge. The test was replaced by the manhunt, and a quantifiable scientific statement was replaced by a hypothesis. At this early stage, this new tracking technique depended on the charisma and almost prophetic intuition of individual forensic psychologists such as James Brussel. It was not until the end of the 1970s that "criminal profiles," as they are now known, were formulated in a systematic manner, and this development took place at a newly established division of the FBI called the "Behavioral Science Unit." Here, psychologists and criminologists were tasked with testing new methods in response to the rising crime rate in the United States. Ever since the 1960s, according to the FBI, not only had the number of unsolved murders been growing – statistics showed that cases in which the offender was unknown to the victim had increased from 10 to 30 percent of the total. Richard Ault and James Reese, whose foundational essay on the new method appeared in the in-house journal, the *FBI Law Enforcement Bulletin*, made the following observation: "As the crime rate grows in this country and the criminals become more sophisticated, the investigative tools of the police officer must also become more sophisticated. One such sophisticated tool ... is the psychological assessment of crime – profiling."[10]

According to Ault and Reese, profiling would enable detectives to decipher the behavioral patterns and motives of criminals on the basis of clues left behind at the scenes of unsolved violent crimes. One of the directors of the Behavioral Science Unit summarized this strategy concisely: "Knowing 'why' will often tell us 'who.'"[11] From the state of the crime scene, detectives could tell whether the offender's methods were organized or unorganized, and on the basis of this simple difference they could begin to narrow down the possible identity of the unknown criminal. Did he live in the immediate vicinity of the victim? Would his apartment be messy or clean? Were they dealing with an eloquent or socially excluded perpetrator? White or black? Fat or skinny (forensic psychologists were convinced that certain mental illnesses manifested themselves in ascetic eating behavior)? At the beginning of their pioneering article, Ault and Reese claim that a series of seven rapes, each with the same recognizable modus operandi, could be solved within a week after the creation of a criminal profile. The latter might contain some of the following conjectured information: "1) The perpetrator's race, 2) Sex, 3) Age range, 4) Marital status, 5) General employment, 6) Reaction to questioning by police, 7) Degree of sexual maturing, 8) Whether the individual might strike again, 9) The possibility that he/she has committed a similar offense in the past, 10) Possible police record."[12]

In 1980, the FBI's *Law Enforcement Bulletin* was devoted entirely to this new form of tracking. Ault and Reese's article is followed by several others in which the concept of the criminal profile is applied specifically to cases of arson or sexual violence. Moreover, the staff of the Behavioral Science Unit began to conduct a long-term series of psychological interviews with convicted mass murderers. In all of this, the ambition to distill individual mental features from a series of crimes was inextricably tied to the presumed illness of the offender in question. As early as 1962, Louis Gold remarked: "It is generally accepted that a person who sets a fire intentionally is committing an abnormal act. His reasoning at this time is perverse, distorted.... The roots of such perverse and aberrant behavior are deep within the personality and have some relationship to sexual disturbance."[13] Ault and Reese likewise underscored the following point: "It is most important that this investigative technique be confined chiefly to crimes against the person where the motive is lacking and where there is sufficient data to recognize the presence of psychopathology at the crime scenes."[14] Profiles were thus created only when no apparent meaning could be derived from the crime itself; on the basis of chaotic crime scenes, they were meant to bring to light the rationality and comparability that the wild rage of the perpetrator had initially obscured. "Psychological profiling," as Anthony Rider noted about arsonists in particular, "should be applied only to those cases in which the unknown subject demonstrates some form of mental, emotional, or behavioral disturbance in the crime. Unless there is perceptible psychopathology present in the crime, a profile cannot be rendered on an unknown subject."[15]

For the FBI, the condition of possibility for the criminal profile was thus the insanity of the offender. The number of cases in which this new method was applied in the United States grew rapidly (in 1979 there were only 65, and in 1980 this number already surpassed 200), while in Germany the first criminal profile – commissioned, incidentally, by the FBI – was created in 1984.[16] The method did not receive widespread public attention, however, until the beginning of the 1990s, and this was largely due to the film *The Silence of the Lambs*, in which an FBI agent trained in psychology manages to convict a serial killer. In the wake of this movie, the work of the "profiler" became a phenomenon of popular culture. A few veterans from the Behavioral Science Unit, such as Robert Ressler and John Douglas, published successful memoirs, and their type of activity has since become a fundamental component of numerous crime shows on television, among them *Criminal Minds*, *Millennium*, *Cracker*, and *Profiler*.

What a brief conceptual history of the profile reveals at once is the fact that, for an entire century, this format has been used to describe individuals in situations involving tests or manhunts. In light of Foucault's fundamental insight that, since the late eighteenth century, knowledge about human beings has been generated predominantly by marginal subjects – that the question of how to track down identities or measure bodies was driven above all by the psychiatric registration of the sick and by the police's access to criminals – it can be said that this trend was consolidated in the knowledge format of the profile. Its object was someone under evaluation or being hunted, and its creators were representatives of state authority, police authority, or scientific authority. In the profiles of the twentieth century, the relations of institutional power were realized with particular clarity. To this extent, the success stories of psychiatry and criminology can be told alongside the genesis of their registration and recording techniques.[17]

Even in the term's older semantic contexts, this constellation is already present. In its art-historical sense as a side view, the word "profile" had been used since the second half of the eighteenth century when attempts were made to systematize and classify certain categories of knowledge through representations of the human face. In the work of Johann Caspar Lavater, the silhouette in profile was transformed from a leisurely form of art into a cryptographic system whose proper interpretation could unlock the inner life of any man or woman. In his treatise *On Physiognomy*, which first appeared in 1772, Lavater left no doubt that portraits ought to depict the side of the face. As evidence for this thesis, he compared a physiognomically relevant profile drawing by Montesquieu with a less revealing portrait and declared that, in the latter, "the view of the painter, and thus the action of the muscles [...] does not present to us the natural condition but rather something that is largely forced, stiff, or tense." This disadvantage of the frontal perspective is alleviated by profile representations because anyone who allows himself to be drawn in this manner does so, according to Lavater, "in large part because the eye of the painter does not govern him but rather looks upon him more naturally and freely."[18] Profile images thus enable greater objectivity and are therefore better suited for physiognomic interpretation. A century later, a similar argument was made by the Parisian criminologist Alphonse Bertillon when he presented his new system for identifying repeat offenders. This system, which he referred to as "anthropometry," involved a series of bodily measurements that were supplemented by profile photographs of delinquents. "It is the profile with precise lines," according to Bertillon, "that best represents the particular individuality of any given face."[19] He believed that this was the case because of the highly identifiable nature of the ear, the form of which differs from person to person and cannot be obscured by any changes of expression while a photograph is being taken. Lavater's and Bertillon's observations make it clear that, as a side view, the profile provided types of knowledge about analyzed and classified subjects that are similar to the types produced later by the tabular and written format with the same name.[20]

The triumph of the self-made profile

The establishment of digital culture over the past quarter-century was accompanied by a massive redefinition and expansion of this format. Whereas Rossolimo's intelligence tests and the FBI's tracking methods were concerned with recording deviant behavior, the objective of today's profiles is largely to underscore the particular attractiveness, competence, or social integration of the person represented. As the debate over the media behavior of the mass murderers from 2012 demonstrated, the format now represents the normal instead of the pathological. How did this shift come about? In which contexts did the coerced personal description transform into something voluntarily created?

In the mid-1990s, when networked and interactive computers spread beyond the confines of American military authorities and hackers to become the global form of communication known as the internet, the technological conditions for creating public spheres changed in a fundamental way. The rapid growth of the "world wide web" and of commercial browsers such as Netscape made it possible for every user to publicize his or her own persona without engaging with the mass media's costly means of production. From the beginning, online "communication" meant not only the acceleration of exchanges between known people (i.e. the transition from letters or faxes to email) but also the ability to address previously unknown people via forums and platforms on the internet.

It was in this new and digital public sphere that the first traces of self-made profiles appeared. For instance, the website Match.com, which today has more than 30 million registered users, began its operations as the first online-dating platform at the beginning of 1995. The earliest version of the site contained the following advice: "Become a member by registering and placing your profile." In an advertisement from 1996, moreover, the company boasted: "Match.com features engaging member profiles."[21] In recent years, the sociologist

Eva Illouz has written extensively on the operating principles of online dating on Match.com and similar sites and has also focused on the profile as a format of self-representation. When registering, users have to answer dozens of questions about their physical appearance, interests, lifestyle, and values in order to provide other members with enough information about themselves and to furnish Match.com's psychologists with a sufficient amount of standardizable material. The hope of finding a "match" among the multitude of potential partners is synonymous with compatibility of two profiles. In her studies, Illouz is primarily interested in the ambivalence of the platforms between intimacy and marketability, between the exposure and commodification of individuals.[22] Regarding the genealogy of the profile concept, Illouz's research, which extends back to the turn of the millennium, is significant if only because it demonstrates how early on this format had established itself as the central form of representing the self in online dating. Only a few years before, the profile was still exclusively known as an instrument for monitoring delinquent subjects, yet in the world of online dating it quickly revealed its greater productive potential as a site for self-description.

Two years after Match.com's IPO in January of 1997, a lawyer named Andrew Weinreich introduced his idea for a website called SixDegrees.com. The goal of this site was not to bring together possible romantic partners but rather to build up a network of friends and acquaintances. Weinreich's presentation is preserved in a grainy YouTube video that, as of the fall of 2018, had attracted a mere 31 views. Such neglect is rather astounding because it is safe to say that this speech represents social media's moment of birth (at least as the term is understood today). Active from 1997 to 2001, SixDegrees was an online network that grew to 3.5 million users and 150 employees but, because of the slow and immobile internet connections of the late 1990s and the limitation of available data to texts, failed to generate lasting attention. This was quite unlike Friendster and Facebook – founded in 2002 and 2003, respectively – whose users had increasing access to broadband internet and digital cameras, and which thus mark the first chapter of social media's global success story.

Weinreich began his speech with the following remarks: "Networking today is the same as it was ten years ago, as it was fifty years ago, as it was a hundred years ago. Today we hope to change that. Today we hope to make history and change how networking works."[23] This confident announcement is followed by a presentation of the SixDegrees website, which did in fact contain all of the basic elements of the subsequent, epoch-shaping social media platforms. At its heart were the profiles of its users. Even though we now tend to associate this format with the billions of self-descriptions on Facebook, LinkedIn, or Instagram, it is certainly possible to identify a sort of prototype in the idea behind SixDegrees.[24] This prototype is described in minute detail in a patent with the title "Method and Apparatus for Constructing a Networking Database and System," which Weinreich and his collaborators submitted on the day that the SixDegrees website went live. The importance of the category of the profile to this system is apparent in the fact that the patented computer program required new users to register by "providing certain requested information." Without such information, the network would not be able to function; new "friends" could not be added, and it would be impossible to search for people with certain characteristics. In a section of the patent titled "Editing Personal Profile," it is stressed once more that, having registered, "the user may list various personal and professional information including e-mail address(es), last name, first name, aliases, occupation, geography, hobbies, skills or expertise, and the like." The abundance of information about each user went hand in hand with SixDegrees's stated business model, which was to offer "an e-mail service wherein a user is assigned an e-mail address in exchange for a profile describing themselves and their tastes." The plan was for every user of SixDegrees to receive individually tailored advertisements on his or her personal page.[25]

In this proto-program of social media from 1997, the profile was thus something from which the business hoped to turn a profit. The service could only be offered for free because its users would indirectly pay for it with a self-made biographical sketch that would provide potential advertisers with previously unknown information about their lives. From the beginning, then, profiles have had two sides in the history of social media: for members, they have provided a free and flexible format of self-representation, while for businesses they have served as a lucrative reservoir containing a wealth of information about real people – real consumers. Exactly how high the economic expectations were for this reservoir became clear when, in 1999, Weinreich and his business partners expressed that the patent would be put up for sale by the new owners of the SixDegrees website. The auction, which took place in 2003, prompted a bidding war for the program among social media pioneers and entrepreneurs in related businesses. Having won the auction with a bid of $700,000, Reid Hoffmann, the co-owner of a recently founded network called LinkedIn, referred to his purchase as a "seminal social-networking patent" that could provide economic and technological guidelines for the development of his own enterprise.[26]

It is worth dwelling on the fact that Weinreich had given his platform, which he thought would revolutionize the possibilities of social networking and could possibly contain "hundreds of thousands, if not millions, of individuals,"[27] the name "SixDegrees." In 1997, this term had a familiar ring to it because it featured in a social-networking thought experiment that had recently gained popularity through the traditional media of theatre and film. In 1990, a play titled *Six Degrees of Separation* debuted in a small theatre on Broadway. The piece went on to become a big success in the United States and was made into an acclaimed movie in 1993. With the title of his website, Weinreich was thus referring to the popular hypothesis at the time that, through friends of friends, any two people could be linked in six steps or fewer.[28] In John Guare's play and in the film, this experiment is carried out through the example of two married couples in New York, both of whom fall victim to a con-artist claiming to be Sydney Poitier's son and a close friend of their children at Harvard. The rest of the plot follows the couples as they attempt to figure out the identity of the unknown man and his mysterious relationship with their sons and daughters, who claim never to have heard of him before. From today's perspective, the work mostly seems like a case study of how to generate knowledge under pre-digital conditions, for all of the questions that search engines and social media can now resolve with a few clicks – Does Sydney Poitier have a son? Who is part of our children's circle of friends? – have to be answered by the swindled families through protracted consultations with traditional media: by means of an autobiography of Poitier bought at a used bookstore, student yearbooks at Harvard, and ultimately the *New York Times*, in which a journalist known to one of the couples writes an article about the con-artist's methods.

Weinreich was thus quite precise in choosing the name "SixDegrees" for the first online network of friends. After all, the contingency and frustrating evasiveness of social relations that gave the play its title could now, thanks to new communication technology, be restrained and used productively to at least the second degree. The format for organizing this confounding web of relations was the profile: a simple personal description that quickly and conveniently made every member identifiable to his or her circle of acquaintances. In the age of social media, the notion of the profile implicitly suggests that a con-man pretending to be Sydney Poitier's son would be found out in a matter of seconds. Even in this era of affirmative self-description, that is, the profile can still be useful to the police. The six degrees of separation between any two people, which on the eve of the digitalization of social relations could still drive the plot of a dark tale of deception, are now becoming transparent and traceable.

Profiles and the culture of job applications

Although the self-made profile first appeared during the second half of the 1990s on social networks and online dating sites, the format soon emerged in a context that was not truly related to the new medium of the internet. In the genre of job-application manuals, which have been flourishing on the book market in conjunction with the gradual standardization of "job-application culture," the concept quickly gained enormous popularity. In Germany, the books by Christian Püttjer and Uwe Schnierda have occupied a dominant position in such literature for the past 25 years. By now, the duo has produced more than 60 guidebooks of this sort, with titles such as *Confidence in Interviews*, *Success in the Assessment Center*, or *The Definitive Job-Application Handbook* (their magnum opus).[29]

These books and brochures began to attribute an important role to the concept of the profile by the end of the 1990s. In their 1999 handbook *Applications and Resumés for College Graduates*, for instance, the authors stressed that "lacking a profile" was the most detrimental factor for applicants, and in a section called "The Rules of Persuasion" they advised job-seekers especially to "create an individual profile."[30] In these early publications, however, the concept did not yet serve as the keyword and foundation of their entire approach to applying for jobs. This changed around the turn of the millennium, when Püttjer and Schnierda trademarked their so-called "profile method" and began to include this term in the titles or subtitles of most of their books.[31] According to Christian Püttjer, their focus on the profile was a response to a media-technical shift in the job market – namely the establishment, around the year 2000, of online job applications – which resulted in the implementation of stricter formal standards and limited the space allowed for narrative elements in covering letters.[32] "The modern requirements for job applications," or so begins *The Definitive Job-Application Handbook*, "can only be met by creating a profiled presentation of oneself." Every stage of a job search is now organized according to this basic category: "Show your profile when making personal contact with potential employers, make sure that it occupies a clear place in your job-application portfolio, present it in phone calls with the businesses you would like to join, and seamlessly integrate it into your interviews."[33] Across the 550 pages of the book, the term recurs in numerous variations: "qualification profile," "job profile," "application profile," "short profile," and so on.

Yet how, in Püttjer and Schnierda's estimation, does an "individual profile brimming with informative keywords" have to look in order for job-seekers to "achieve their goal and find a desirable position?" The three "cornerstones" of the profile method, which the authors list at the beginning of every publication, seem rather ambivalent in certain respects. The third point – "trustworthiness" – contains the following exhortation: "Do not distort yourself; your personality is in demand!" And yet this injunction to represent yourself as authentically as possible contradicts the first point, which requires the "precise fit" of applicants and makes the following claim: "The more you cater to the stated job requirements in your application, the more likely you will be to succeed. Adopt the perspective of the HR department."[34] This dual challenge – the conflict between honest introspection and adapting oneself to suit the needs of others – is perhaps indicative of a fundamental characteristic of the self-made profile: it is a format that simultaneously allows for both the utmost individuality and the utmost conformity.

To the extent that the goal of self-description is to suit the prescribed requirements of an employer as closely as possible, today's independently created profiles approximate those created in the name of applied psychology and criminology. In job-application profiles, the external perspective of the psychologist or criminal investigator, which was directed toward pathological schoolchildren or unknown offenders, has simply been transferred to the authors themselves. They must be able to view themselves with the unerring eyes of the businesses where they might want to work. In this light, it makes sense that Püttjer and Schnierda offer the following advice to those creating profiles: "Become a detective on your own case and uncover your professional past!"[35] Thus, the application specialists themselves imply that criminal investigation can serve as a fitting model for representing oneself on the job market. Today's profiles, though composed in a gesture of sovereign individuality, conform to a prescribed set of requisites, and it is presumably this very conflict that gave rise to the contradictory metaphors in Püttjer and Schnierda's guidebooks. As the authors repeatedly stress, profiles need to have "sharp contours," and yet they also urge applicants to "round out their profiles."[36] The incoherence of this imagery demonstrates the paradoxical demands of the format. Representing a unique yet fully adaptable individual, the ideal profile has to be precisely and imprecisely delineated at the same time.

Constants of external control

Today, more than 20 years after the arrival of social media and the firm establishment of job-application guides, the profile is an unchallenged and omnipresent form of subjectivization. On the job market, networks such as LinkedIn or Xing, which have millions of members, have made it a structural necessity for professional self-representations to be created in the form of online profiles. In a milieu like the university, every academic homepage, every research proposal, and every project description now has to be accompanied by an impressive "researcher profile" or "applicant profile." As discussed above, the creation and maintenance of personal profiles on social media have become indicators of sound mental health. The format thus appears in both professional and private spheres as a faithful and autonomously manageable representative of the self, and people can constantly be heard talking about their own profiles.

This success story, however, not only disguises the historical fact that the format was developed as a normalizing and disciplinary instrument. It also diverts attention away from the present reality that, in tandem with the triumph of self-made profiles, the format has become a more effective means of describing and controlling others than ever before. In digital culture, the novel effects of profiles in the formation of the subject are offset by the multifaceted tendency to treat individuals as the object of standardized and interconnected data acquisition. Concepts such as the "user profile," "personality profile," or "customer profile" involve not only the actively and voluntarily divulged data *of* the user but also information *about* the user that has been collected, largely without notice, by companies, authorities, and agencies. The latter practice – a technique from surveying and census-taking – is, of course, far older than the recent history of self-generated profiles.[37]

Over the past 15 years, a central stage for this method has been marketing. Before the establishment of social networks, the ability to address potential customers depended entirely on the crude and unilateral channels of mass media. Advertisements in newspapers, on the radio, or on television thus had the same form for all readers, listeners, or viewers, and the impact of a company's new slogan or campaign was tied to the hope that the creative genius of the advertising agency could capture the attention of the widest possible circle of consumers. Through the fragmentation of the media system in digital culture, in which every user is simultaneously a consumer and producer, the anonymous masses have transformed into a multitude of individually addressable people. Under these new technological conditions, "marketing" means defining smaller and smaller target groups and even, in the ideal case, addressing individual customers with customized information. In this communicative situation, the profile is the place where advertisers can gather and evaluate information about their addressees.

The relationship between businesses and targeted consumers resembles that between forensic psychology and criminals, and marketing specialists have themselves noticed this and even emphasized the point. Since 2003, for instance, the German business consultant Andreas Wenzlau has offered a service called *KundenProfiling* ("Customer Profiling"), which he derived from the somewhat older American concept of "consumer profiling."[38] The logo used on his website and on his self-published handbook is thus an enlarged fingerprint. In the preface to the latter work, Wenzlau claims that he compared "the structures of criminological profiling with today's marketing practices" and discovered "very interesting parallels." "While wrestling with questions concerning customers, acquisition, and marketing," he goes on, "I was struck by an idea: New methods and options would be needed to understand the actual motives of consumers. *It would have to become possible to enter the customers' minds!*"[39] The term "customer profiling," however, is an explicit expression of what has become a fundamental business model in the digital age of search engines, social networks, and online services. As is well known, global firms such as Google and Facebook have built their empires on the promise, first formulated by Andrew Weinreich, that companies are able to tailor, with previously unthinkable flexibility, the form and frequency of their advertisements for individual users. In 2007, for instance, Google patented a controversial method that enabled the company to construct reliable "user profiles" from the behavior of computer game players. Along with a player's individual tactics, the amount of time he or she spends on a gaming platform supposedly provides insights into the user's consumer preferences and thus enables highly effective advertisements to be placed at specific points in time.[40]

Over the past 15 years, the fact that companies possess such profile-based knowledge has provoked specific questions concerning data protection. In a country such as Germany, which has complex legal provisions governing "informational self-determination," the development of the profile format was greeted with critical commentary from early on. As early as the year 2000, in an article on the use of personality profiles for marketing purposes, the lawyer Petra Wittig formulated grave "legal objections" against this form of data processing, and she stressed her conviction that even the consent of customers would do nothing to change the problematic nature of such a practice. The individual right to self-determination loses its validity, according to Wittig, "when personal integrity is placed without restriction at the disposal of those interested in data." The creation of "user profiles" in marketing would therefore have to be forbidden in principle on the basis of the fundamental right to "informational self-determination."[41] Despite this early criticism, however, the precise legal status of the format was slow to be defined. As Christoph Schnabel noted in his 2009 dissertation on data protection and the concept of the profile, "there has yet to be a single case of legislation in which the creation of a profile has been treated as unlawful." As of 2009, according to Schnabel, the format of the user profile did not even qualify as a "legal concept"[42] – a loophole that was not closed until recently. In May, 2018, the European Union's long-discussed "General Data Protection Regulation," which attempts to strike a balance between free trade and legal stability, finally came into effect. This regulation, which unifies the previously heterogeneous legislation of the individual member states, provides the terms "profile" and "profiling" with their first legal definition. They consist of "any form of automated processing of personal data evaluating the personal aspects relating to a natural person, in particular to analyze or predict aspects concerning the data subject's performance at work, economic situation, health, personal preferences or interests, reliability or behaviour, location or movements." Among the "principles of fair and transparent processing" of personal data, EU regulations now "require that the data subject be informed of the existence of the processing operation and its purposes."[43]

The authors of this legislation were aware, however, that the knowledge in profiles is not simply being collected by companies but is also being produced by the individual users themselves. A preliminary remark thus states: "This Regulation does not apply to the processing of personal data by a natural person in the course of a purely personal or household activity and thus with no connection to a professional or commercial activity." Such activity might include, for instance, "social networking."[44] Aside from the fact that this stipulation maintains the fragile boundary between "personal" and "professional" activity online, the permeability of which has engendered many ways of economizing private life in digital culture, this passage does much to underscore the ambivalence of the current concept of the profile. For data protectionists, the superimposed "profile" is never fully congruent with the core of an individual's legally protected "personality." Profiling is regarded as an external act of attribution, a fact that led Schnabel in 2009 to the conviction that, "as regards profiles, the self-determination of consumers is, from an economic perspective, diametrically opposed to the interests of businesses."[45]

This constellation has since changed entirely. By way of their profiles, users of social media now endeavor on a daily basis to depict their own personality in a congruent manner, and in this act of self-determination they provide businesses and advertisers with a constant stream of information. Passive and active access to the format has yielded a remarkable alliance that can no longer be understood in terms of the traditional categories of data protection. In today's profiles on Facebook, LinkedIn, or Instagram, self-representation and external control – subjectivization and objectivization – are blending together in an inextricable manner, and we are only gradually beginning to see what new sorts of social and political spheres might arise from this alliance. Though less than 20 years old, in any case, Petra Wittig's suggestion that even the voluntary creation of profiles should be prohibited by law sounds like something from a distant era.

The American psychologist Michal Kosinski has assembled a wealth of evidence regarding the proximity of autonomous creation and external evaluation in today's profiles. Since 2011, he and his colleagues have published a number of articles concerned with making reliable statements about people by applying the methods of personality psychology to Twitter or Facebook profiles. Kosinski's analyses are based on the so-called "big-five" or "five-factor" model, which, since Lewis Goldberg's work in the late 1980s, has been a significant testing procedure in the field. The big-five model divides individual feelings and emotions into five basic traits and aims to determine, by means of a standardized set of questions, the relationship among these traits in the behavior of the person being tested. In this way, it hopes to construct a taxonomy of the human personality. Kosinski's much-discussed thesis is that such knowledge can be obtained far more quickly and with the same level of precision by analyzing profiles on social networks. In his first article, from 2011, he demonstrated with a small cohort of a few hundred users that the most important elements of a Twitter profile – its number of followers, the number of accounts followed by the user, and the number of tweets – were sufficient for determining someone's personality traits according to the five-factor model, and that the conclusions drawn in this manner corresponded to those determined in actual analyses with a probability greater than 90 percent. Twitter profiles, in other words, could be used to make reliable predictions about the personality types of the users in question – whether they are more or less "reserved," "conscientious," "agreeable," "cooperative," or "sensitive."[46]

In the following years, Kosinski and his colleagues expanded the scope of their investigation by inviting, on a Facebook page called "myPersonality," hundreds of thousands of social media users to take a big-five personality test, and then they compared these results with the users' profiles. In 2013, they published a study that analyzed the personality types of around 60,000 subjects in light of their "likes" on Facebook – that is, their affirmational responses to comments or to shared products, texts, pictures, and videos. "We show," the authors claim, "that easily accessible digital records of behavior, Facebook Likes, can be used to automatically and accurately predict a range of highly sensitive personal attributes including: sexual orientation, ethnicity, religious and political views, ... age, and gender."[47] From the behavior discernible from a user's profile, according to the article, the authors were able to determine with 90-percent accuracy whether the person in question was hetero- or homosexual, and with about 85-percent accuracy whether he or she voted for Republicans or Democrats.

In the abstract of his 2013 study, Kosinski stresses that it is primarily the "easily accessible" nature of the data that makes his method so attractive in comparison with the complex methods of personality analyses conducted by school psychologists.[48] Thanks to the ease of acquiring data from profiles, this sort of research, he concludes, "suggests future directions in a variety of areas, including" – especially – the world of "*Marketing*."[49] This direction would in fact be pursued in a manner that was presumably never taken into consideration by academic psychologists. At the end of 2016, the British firm Cambridge Analytica began to attract widespread media attention for having possibly influenced the US presidential election in favor of Donald Trump. The belief was that the company had made use of Kosinski's profile analytics to send individually tailored Facebook messages to certain voters, and that these messages helped to bring about the unexpected result in the election. At an election event in the summer of 2016, Cambridge Analytica's CEO Alexander Nix made the following claim: "If you know the personality of the people you are targeting, you can nuance your messaging to resonate more effectively with those key audience groups."[50] Following Kosinski's example, the company invited millions of potential voters to participate in a personality test on Facebook, and from the results of this test it determined the focus and content of the messages in question.

In the spring of 2018, it was ultimately revealed that Cambridge Analytica had silently accessed nearly 90 million Facebook profiles between 2014 and 2016 – a scandal that brought Mark Zuckerberg to the floor of the US Senate and incited a long debate between journalists and media theorists about the actual influence of so-called "target profiling" on the outcome of recent elections. Yet, regardless of how deeply the political marketing by Cambridge Analytica and comparable agencies affected the behavior of voters, the fact remains that Kosinski's analyses have shown, with particular clarity, the extent to which the profile oscillates between autonomy and external control. With a rather old-fashioned term of political critique, it would be possible to refer to the activity of target profiling as "voter manipulation." Regarding the forms of subjectivization in digital culture, however, it is characteristic that this intervention was choreographed by means of the very format which, for a good ten years, most people had considered a sovereign space for self-representation.

Cyberspace and profiles: from the boundless to the captive self

The dominant role of the profile in digital culture is also instructive because the profile established a representational form of the self that could be understood as antithetical to the concepts of the subject that prevailed during the early age of the internet. In the mid-1990s, diagnoses of a new media era typically included a great deal of emphatic talk about the self and its novel developmental possibilities within the virtual sphere of the internet. In their discussions of online forms of subjectivization, influential authors at the time such as Howard Rheingold, Sherry Turkle, John Perry Barlow, or Nicholas Negroponte focused on the medium's lack of boundaries and on aspects of masquerading and multiplicity. Referring to role-playing games such as *Dungeons and Dragons*, for instance, Turkle repeatedly stressed that online identity is "not only decentered but multiplied without limit."[51] The subject of users, she thought, had to be understood through categories such as "difference, multiplicity, heterogeneity, and fragmentation."[52] "When we live through our electronic self-representations," according to Turkle, "we have unlimited possibilities to be *many*."[53] Howard Rheingold, who coined the term "virtual community" in the early 1990s, likewise made a case that our identities are "fluid" on the internet; he discusses the activity that took place on early networks such as the "Whole Earth 'Lectronic Link," whose members, like the role players described by Turkle, were registered under nicknames, and thus their identities could be concealed or multiplied.[54] The fluidity of the online self is also a central argument of the most prominent manifesto from the early age of the internet, John Perry Barlow's "A Declaration of the Independence of Cyberspace," which was published in

February 1996: "Our identities have no bodies, so, unlike you, we cannot obtain order by physical coercion."[55] These words were written in response to the Telecommunications Act enacted by Bill Clinton, which stipulated greater regulation and oversight over online content. During the pioneering days of digital culture, in short, the subject was thought to be a fluid and amorphous category.

This attitude was reflected in the spatial metaphors used to describe the internet at the time, including the concept of "cyberspace," which Barlow had borrowed and redefined from William Gibson's novel *Neuromancer*. Cyberspace promised to be an egalitarian and immaterial space that was free from state and police intervention – "beyond government control," as Fred Turner remarked in his book about the rise of digital utopias in California.[56] Barlow, who, like many of the movement's pioneering figures, came from the Californian counterculture, associated these fantasies about the unconstrained nature of virtual identities and spaces with LSD experiences during the 1960s and 1970s. He believed that the boundless online world would, like LSD, enable a psychedelic trip – one caused not by synthetic drugs but by information technology: "The computer itself was a new LSD."[57] In Barlow's estimation, the important and utopian quality of this sphere lay in the fact that it could not be delineated and controlled, a characteristic that would give rise to a second spatial metaphor for the internet at the time: the electronic frontier. Just as nineteenth-century immigrants to the United States kept pushing westward, the early users of the internet were constantly entering unmapped territory where the inhabitants could express, according to Barlow's "Declaration," their "authentic identity."[58]

Over the past 20 years, such fantasies about a fluid and multiple self in boundless space have obviously faded away. An entirely different concept – an entirely different genealogy of the internet and its collective subjects – has since taken their place. The profile, which began to appear on online-dating sites and in job-application culture around the same time as Rheingold's, Turkle's, or Barlow's eloquent theories, opposed these dreams of fluidity as a format that is oriented entirely around structure, predictability, and standardization. In the central methods of self-representation and self-perception that have since been established in digital culture, the subject and his or her space exist to be ascertained. To illustrate the gulf between these two concepts, all that is needed is to compare the passionate arguments from the 1990s in favor of the multiple self with the guidelines governing today's largest social network and its 2 billion active members. The section titled "Registration and Account Security" in Facebook's "Statement of Rights and Responsibilities" begins with the following injunction: "Facebook users provide their real name and information." Other "responsibilities" that every member must accept when registering include: "You will not provide any false personal information on Facebook," "You will not create more than one personal account," and "You will keep your contact information accurate and up-to-date."[59]

Facebook's founder, Mark Zuckerberg, has himself stressed that the spectacular success of his business and its triumph over early competitors such as MySpace are in large part due to his insistence on the uniform and unambiguous identity of the site's users. In his interviews with the journalist David Kirkpatrick, which were published in 2010, he interpreted MySpace's indifference to the number and genuine nature of its users' profiles as a decisive weakness and a target to attack: "MySpace was unconcerned with who you really were."[60] His own flourishing network, in contrast, required from the beginning that each user could only have one profile and that it had to be under his or her real name. "You have one identity," Zuckerberg repeatedly maintained in the interviews, and he spoke of the "lack of integrity" associated with the multiple and fictitious profiles created on MySpace.[61] According to his credo, "You can't be on Facebook without being your authentic self!"[62] Of course, the reasons for this insistence on authenticity were more commercial than philosophical, given that, from the outset, the business has been able to provide advertisers with a lucrative supply of real names and addresses. Regarding the conception of humanity in digital culture and the disappearance of the early discourse about the multiple subject, however, this mantra of the "authentic self" represents a threshold: the anonymous or disguised ego has given way to an ego that is readily identifiable. Just a few years after its announcement, Barlow's fluid category of "authentic identity" in cyberspace congealed into something that could not be better suited for police surveillance.

In his book *From Counterculture to Cyberculture*, Fred Turner framed the transitional process under discussion between two historical turning points: the campus protests at Berkeley in 1964, where students wore IBM punch cards around their necks to symbolize their powerlessness against the machinery of the university, and the publication of manifestos such as Negroponte's *Being Digital* and Barlow's "Declaration of the Independence of Cyberspace" in the mid-1990s. Turner's main objective was to explore how, within a period of 30 years, information technology was able to develop from a menacing and subject-inhibiting force into a sphere of social utopia and individual liberation. My considerations here about the status of the self in digital culture have described how this transformation has both progressed and regressed in recent years – developments that Turner, who completed his book before the advent of social media, could not have taken into account. For it ranks among the most irritating features of the current relation between subject formation and digital media technology that the promises of freedom declaimed during the pioneering years of the internet continue to provide the ideological basis of all new devices and services (every Apple presentation and every expansion of the sharing culture is an echo of the "virtual community"), while the methods of individualization – as shown by the development of the profile concept – are no longer intended to scatter subjects but rather to arrest them.

2

Locations: GPS and the Aesthetics of Suspicion

The initial novelty of cellular phones was their mobility. In their present incarnation as "smartphones," however, they are also defined by their ability to be located. These small hand-held devices no longer simply serve as tools for making telephone calls, sending messages, or browsing the internet – they also trace and disclose our whereabouts. The prefix "smart" that has been associated with our phones for more than a decade happens to designate, above all, the device's capacity to allow others to track down its owner. To use a smartphone is to overcome space and map it at the same time.

The great degree to which location technologies have shaped the services of today's mobile phones becomes evident in a quick glance at the colorful mosaic of icons arranged on their screens. Among the pre-installed and undeletable symbols are those for services such as "maps" or "weather," which indicate the geographical position of the user. A small icon toward the top of the screen, which looks like a compass, can be pressed at any time to reveal whether the location function is active or not. In order to see the complete selection of such "location-based services" and their control settings, however, it is necessary to delve into layers of the operating system that are seldom encountered during daily use. These can only be exposed by way of something like a "close reading" of the mobile phone. On the iPhone 5s, for instance, which is one of the most popular smartphones in circulation, a sequence of taps from the "settings" icon to "privacy" and then to "location services" will lead to a place where this function can be switched on or off and where it is possible to view a list of all the pre-installed or independently uploaded applications that can determine one's location. At the end of this list, a category called "system services" leads to an additional selection of the iPhone's internal location functions – for instance, to the service "frequent locations," which lists the user's most visited places (by address, date, and time) and pinpoints them on city maps. Here, six levels deeper into the iOS operating system than the basic "settings" icon, the device displays a protocol of its user's movements over the course of the last six weeks or so – a sort of "auto-geography." In an official statement titled "About Location Services and Privacy," Apple makes the following remark about these features: "[Y]our iOS device will keep track of places you've recently been, as well as how often and when you visited them. This data is kept solely on your device ... It will be used to provide you with personalized services, such as predictive traffic routing."[1]

The methods used for locating individuals have a genealogy that closely resembles that of the conceptual and functional history of the profile. In this case, too, an instrument of knowledge that was recently restricted to policing has since become, in digital culture, an omnipresent and even humdrum aspect of everyday life. What were the conditions at the end of the twentieth century that gave rise to the constant practice of identifying and tracking a person's position from afar? Not even 20 years ago, the technical challenges, costs, and legal complications involved with such an undertaking could only be justified in the case of people who were suspected of planning heinous crimes. (Crime movies and cop shows released around the year 2000 all seem to have a scene in which the detectives, having planted a tracking device in the suspect's car, are now sitting back in their office or patrol car and watching a little beeping symbol as it scurries across a stylized map of the city.)

On today's smartphones, this same sort of technology is constantly in use, whether in the case of internal services such as "maps" or "frequent locations" or in any variety of uploaded applications for ordering a taxi or dinner, reserving the nearest car-sharing option, reviewing a restaurant, saving the address of a new favorite bar, or meeting another person for a night out (or the rest of one's life). MyTaxi, Uber, Lieferando, Drive Now, Yelp, Foursquare, Tinder, *Pokémon Go*, Facebook Places – each of these apps has the user's conditional consent to identify his or her exact position, and when you order your first Uber ride, for instance, and watch the little black limousine as it moves on your screen in real time toward your own location, it is almost impossible not to associate this with the activity of police surveillance. Uber transactions are shrouded in an atmosphere of conspiracy: the route of the limousine leaves behind a trail that can be traced back with the utmost precision, and yet it is a trail without a case. The actual event may have been monitored and mapped with criminological means, but no one expects that it will reveal any unfamiliar or previously hidden clues, as would be the hope in a crime investigation. Whereas locating people was once intended to uncover a secret or bring to light an obscure element in their daily routines, this investigative aspect now plays no role at all for the user of today's smartphone apps. The verticality of detective work has transformed into the horizontality of daily tracking, which is now used for the sake of having fun, making money, or meeting romantic partners.

The history of satellite navigation

The ability to determine your whereabouts at any time with your phone depends on a location technology that is now universally and freely available. The technology in question is the satellite-navigation service known as GPS ("global positioning system"), which was developed from 1973 to 1995 by the US Department of Defense and has, since the year 2000, been available without restriction for civilian use as well. When determining its user's position, every smartphone today relies above all on GPS; competing systems such as Russia's GLONAS or the EU-financed GALILEO service are either highly limited in scope or not entirely operational.

The history of satellite navigation begins with the launch of Sputnik 1 in October of 1957, an event that extended the Cold War into outer space. Scientists at Johns Hopkins University's Applied Physics Laboratory, a center for American military research, were soon able to determine the exact location of the enemy's object in space. "After they had demonstrated the effectiveness of their method," according to an early GPS historian, "the next obvious move was to reverse it in order to determine the position of things on earth."[2] The first American satellites, which were launched at the beginning of the 1960s, were designed to enable the military (and, as of 1967, civilians) to track the location of ships. Compared with the technique of radiolocation, which had been in use since the early twentieth century, the new form of navigation had a number of advantages, including less interference, greater precision, simpler data analysis, and a broader operating range.[3]

The first American satellite, however, orbited at a relatively low altitude of around 1,100 kilometers, and this made its navigation system rather unreliable. On account of sporadic visibility, for instance, it could only track ships every hour and a half, and faster vehicles such as airplanes and rockets could not be located at all. For these reasons, the American military began to experiment rather early on with more distant satellites and with different transmission techniques. In 1973, a new program was initiated with the long title "Navigational Satellite Timing and Ranging – Global Positioning System" (NAVSTAR GPS), and this was meant to supplant the earlier system (known as "Transit"). In February 1978, after a testing phase in Arizona, a satellite was launched for the first time to an altitude above 20,000 kilometers; by 1985, ten satellites of the first GPS generation were equipped with integrated atomic clocks. Each of these continuously transmitted, at the speed of light, its position and exact time back to earth. The receiver at ground level was located by coordinating these time signals. In order to determine the longitude, latitude, and altitude of a location, real-time measurements from three satellites were needed, and a fourth was used to correct the difference between the synchronized times of transmission and reception. Altogether, 24 GPS satellites would be needed in various orbits in space in order to provide these four measurements at any place and time and thus to determine the position of a receiver within a few meters of its actual location. When the United States first embarked upon its location project with eight NATO partners (West Germany included), the goal was to have the system fully operational during the second half of the 1980s. The program was stalled for three years, however, on account of the disaster with the Challenger space shuttle at the beginning of 1986. It was not until 1994 that enough satellites were put into orbit to ensure that locations could be determined constantly and around the globe. As of today, 32 GPS satellites are active in space.

Regarding the history and present use of location services, it is significant that GPS was initially developed for military purposes. Friedrich Kittler's famous remark that the everyday use of electronic media is ultimately an "abuse of army equipment" applies just as well to location technology.[4] Throughout the twentieth century, the entire history of knowledge concerned with determining locations has been intertwined with military technology, from the first applications of radar during the First World War and the refinement of radiolocation during the Second World War to the use of satellite navigation at the height of the Cold War. These technologies were meant to locate enemy ships, airplanes, and missiles as early and reliably as possible, and to ensure that one's own weapons would strike their targets with the greatest possible precision. In the earliest studies and reports concerned with the development of GPS, this logic of combat – between the West and the Eastern bloc – defines the rhetoric of the entire discussion: "It is important that the system is secure against enemy interference," states a 1978 article published in the German journal *Ortung und Navigation*, and the author goes on to explain that, "in light of the planned GPS service's astonishingly high number of twenty-four satellites," it would be necessary to ensure "a certain degree of protection against the enemy's predatory satellites." In the same issue of the journal, a representative of the Bureau for Military Technology (Bundesamt für Wehrtechnik) stressed that, in comparison with the Transit system, the new location system would reduce "our susceptibility to the enemy's attempts at deception," and, a few issues later, an admiral expressed that the complete coverage of the earth's orbit with GPS satellites would provide "a high degree of invulnerability."[5] As its developers and these early accounts of GPS make clear, there is little doubt that satellite navigation was above all a technique for latent – or, if necessary, active – warfare. It is thus no surprise that the United States first systematically implemented this location service (even though it was not yet fully operational) during the Gulf War of 1990 and 1991. The main objects to be located were weapons and means of transportation; it was beside the point, at this early stage, that GPS signals might also be used to track human beings.

In addition to such military applications, however, the US Ministry of Defense also took into account the potential civilian and commercial uses of GPS. These services were to be made available through a second radio frequency that could determine locations with far less accuracy. During the initial tests conducted at the beginning of the 1980s, however, this signal in fact proved to be too precise, and thus it had to be artificially weakened from the Air Force's ground control in Colorado. The second frequency, which could identify locations within 100 meters and was known as the "Standard Positioning System," was intended to be made available for the civilian tracking of ships and airplanes, and it differed from the so-called "Precise Positioning Service," which was to be reserved for military use and could locate targets within a range of 10 meters. Thus, a two-tiered system was built into the location service from its earliest planning stages (and so the story, so often told in American histories of GPS, that the 1983 shooting of a Korean passenger plane in Soviet airspace had prompted a "shocked and emotional President Reagan" to equivocate about making the system available for civilian use should be regarded as ideologically motivated and spurious).[6]

In the mid-1990s, when the Global Positioning System was finally able to ensure continuous and universal tracking services, the US Ministry of Defense decided to make the less accurate Standard Positioning Service freely available for civilian use (at least for a trial period of ten years). This measure led to the first attempts to apply GPS technology to such things as surveying land, directing traffic, and navigating airplanes, though the preconditions for more comprehensive applications would not be in place until the government decided to remove the artificial restrictions from the civilian signal. In a presidential directive from 1996, Bill Clinton announced his goal to "encourage acceptance and integration of GPS into peaceful civil, commercial, and scientific applications worldwide ... It is our intention to discontinue the use of GPS Selective Availability (SA) within a decade."[7] The apparent progress of the European Union's navigation system known as GALILEO, which seemed to be prepped for activation by the end of 1999 (it is still not fully operational), impelled the American government to put an abrupt end to its artificial restrictions on the civilian GPS signal: "It's rare," a spokesperson explained at the press conference held on the occasion, "that someone can press a button and make something you own instantly more valuable." The reason why the United States chose to make its location system fully available four years ahead of the planned deadline was related to the economic expectations for the new technology: "Right now," according to another spokesperson at the same press release, "the market for GPS applications and services is in the multibillion range, and it's doubling every two or three years. So it's an enormous market, and we're trying to make sure that U.S. business has an opportunity to move out there."[8] Over the last 15 years, this prediction has turned out to be an underestimation, and the omnipresence of locating methods today has made it easy to forget that every map on a smartphone and every use of Uber, Tinder, or Facebook Places is based on this political decision from the year 2000.

On the way to locating individuals

Since the late twentieth century, the history of location technology has been defined by three main applications: first as a strategic tool during the Cold War, second as an instrument for monitoring and tracking criminals, and third as an everyday form of communication in digital culture. Regarding this gradual expansion of user groups, it would thus also be possible to say that methods for determining locations were first employed exclusively by the military, then primarily by the police and the justice system, and finally, over the past ten years, by every single person who owns a smartphone.

Indications of the first shift – from a tool of war to an instrument for tracking criminals – were detectable from early on. In the late 1960s, and thus still before the advent of GPS technology, systematic efforts were made in the United States to develop something called "Automatic Vehicle Location" in large cities. At this stage, the ability to track the location of motor vehicles and their passengers still depended on costly and limited methods such as the "dead-reckoning" navigation process – which could only determine the position of an object in relation to a known point of departure – the comprehensive installation of control posts (for the automatic collection of tolls, for instance), or radiolocation, which was used at the time to track ships and airplanes. The earliest applications of the latter technique may have been concerned with coordinating public transportation or directing traffic on busy highways, but the idea of using it to monitor criminals was a matter of debate from the beginning. At the so-called PULSE Conference in Washington, DC, which was organized by traffic authorities in 1968 to foster discussion about the so-called "Urban Locator Service," the potential benefits of the system for law enforcement were openly acknowledged: "Another, secretive, law enforcement use of AVM [Automatic Vehicle Monitor] systems would be in 'bugging' suspect vehicles, valuable shipments, etc.; movement could be traced through the city without a conspicuous 'tail.'" "Future refinement of the craft," the speaker went on, "may make it possible to implant a transponder on the subject's person – in his shoe, for instance."[9]

In the 1970s and 1980s, police work joined traffic control as a prominent use of "Automatic Vehicle Location." A research report published by the US Department of Justice in 1976, for instance, names tracking and surveillance as possible "covert" uses of the technology: "Keeping track of the location of containerized freight has been mentioned as a possible application of AVL. Actual requirements as to accuracy and coverage area have not been developed. If a practical technique can be developed which requires no intervention other than the placement of some device in or on the freight container, covert uses become feasible."[10] Drug traffickers and smugglers of contraband, for example, could be apprehended by such means.

Despite these early tracking fantasies, however, it is noteworthy that the location of suspects was initially not the primary application of this technology in the hands of law enforcement. At first, the most urgent goal of the police was to determine, by automatic means, the position of their own fleet of vehicles in order to create a greater sense of safety for the officers on patrol. Early studies devoted to this topic in Germany, too, focused on the potential of location technology to provide "safety" and "optimal organization."[11] It was hoped that the ability to locate positions automatically would, in the future, ease communication between patrol cars and central stations, which had hitherto taken place orally over the radio. In response to this suggestion, the president of the German Police Academy, who was one of the strongest opponents of the new technology, raised the question of whether police officers in tracked patrol cars might feel "monitored, controlled, and excessively supervised."[12] In the decade that gave rise to census boycotts and the "right to informational self-determination" in Germany, even police chiefs were trying to develop a reasonable approach to data storage and location technology.

By the mid-1980s, German authorities had still not located any suspected criminals with technical means. By the same time in the United States, in contrast, this tracking practice had already been implemented regardless of the limited scope and accuracy of the technology. The hope from 1978 that locating procedures "would require no more than a small beeper to be planted on or within the cargo under surveillance" was fulfilled a decade later, at least to the extent that radio transmitters with a range of 100 meters could be furtively attached to the vehicle or belongings of suspects and followed by an undercover patrol car. Historical evidence for the early stages of this practice is preserved in a few rulings by the US Supreme Court, which first had to issue decisions about its legality in the early 1980s. In two similar cases filed in 1983 and 1984, the defendants, who had been convicted of producing illicit drugs on the basis of tracking information from a radio transmitter, contested the legality of such practices. The first case concerned a man named Leroy Knotts, who had been linked to a crime by a tracking device in a container of chloroform, and the second a man named James Karo, whose illegal activity had been established by a tracking device planted on a can of ether.[13]

In the context of investigative work, these practices stood apart because, for the first time, location technology was used to track not simply vehicles or weapons but also individual people. The targets of these efforts, in other words, were human beings. When satellite navigation became available on a limited basis for civilian applications in the mid-1990s, its use in police manhunts soon became more and more common. The inaugural volume of the journal *GPS Solutions*, which came out in 1995, contains an article about potential civilian uses of "real-time tracking," and here the authors consider, among other things, how the technology might be used "to monitor criminals."[14] The police department in Colorado Springs was at that point evaluating, according to the authors, "how GPS technology can help reduce crime and improve the community policing program."[15] The vehicles of suspected drug and contraband smugglers could be continuously monitored with GPS transmitters, thereby reducing the logistical burdens associated with physical manhunts (which, as one police officer remarked, "were some of the most manpower-intensive and costly operations").[16] The covert tracking of a vehicle typically required the involvement of at least five patrol cars to cover the area in question: "The officers felt if they could have a system that could effectively track criminals remotely (out of sight), they would be safer and fewer agents would be required to handle a single case."[17] Since the late 1990s, it has in fact been a standard practice for the police to employ GPS technology in efforts to hunt down and monitor suspected criminals.

Paradoxes of location

Location technologies have had two main areas of application in criminal prosecutions. They have been used to monitor suspects by means of transmitters planted on vehicles or cargo, and they have been used to monitor convicted criminals on probation by means of so-called electronic ankle bracelets or, more recently, GPS-equipped wristbands. If one considers the legal controversy that has surrounded these two applications over the last 30 years, it becomes immediately apparent how much effort has gone into legitimizing the practice of locating suspected or convicted offenders. It has long been a matter of political and legal debate whether the constant surveillance of someone's movements by state authorities should be understood as an excessive invasion of human privacy. This question is of particular interest in light of the frequency and impartiality with which location services are used on today's mobile phones. For a good decade, there has thus been a noteworthy divide in the employment of location methods: on the one hand, their strictly governed use in tracking down delinquents, and, on the other hand, their ubiquitous and casual use by smartphone owners wishing to locate themselves.

From today's perspective, the documents pertaining to the Supreme Court cases mentioned above are instructive because they reveal the many legal complications posed by electronic tracking methods. The lawsuits filed by Knotts (1983) and Karo (1984) concern the question of whether police manhunts aided by tracking devices violate the Fourth Amendment of the US Constitution, which guarantees the "right of the people to be secure in their persons, houses, papers, and effects, against unreasonable searches and seizures." Moreover, it also maintains that any warrant granting such procedures will only be issued "upon probable cause, supported by oath or affirmation, and particularly describing the place to be searched, and the persons or things to be seized." This amendment was added to the American Constitution in 1791, long before the advent and criminological use of technical media, and thus over the course of the twentieth century the Supreme Court has repeatedly had to decide whether certain new and media-enhanced methods of surveillance happen to infringe upon codified personal rights. In the 1928 case *Olmstead* v. *United States*, for instance, the issue was whether wiretapped telephone conversations represented an illegally obtained form of evidence. The Supreme Court ruled in favor of the procedure because the information was not acquired within the protected living space of the suspect but rather in the unprotected space of the telephone lines (at that time, interestingly enough, technical channels such as telephone lines were not yet treated in the law as an extension of private space but rather as a stable connective element between the public and private spheres).[18] The legally confirmed independent existence of the medium, however, would be overturned in an influential Supreme Court ruling from 1967, in which the plaintiff was a convicted criminal named Katz whose conversations in a public phone booth were recorded by a microphone planted on the roof. The judge deemed this practice unconstitutional because, in his estimation, someone using a telephone booth had an expectation of privacy. In legal terms, the act of listening in on someone's conversation with a microphone was thus synonymous with physically intruding into someone's private space. The Fourth Amendment, according to the judge's frequently cited verdict, "protects people, not places."[19]

The ability to locate suspects automatically lent new significance to this confict between a late-eighteenth-century legal text and the tracking technology of the late twentieth century. The cases of Knotts and Karo in the mid-1980s addressed the concrete problem of whether the use of radio transmitters, whose signals could be received by nearby patrol cars, should be considered an "unreasonable search" and thus require an appropriate warrant. The first lawsuit was unanimously dismissed by the judges because the chloroform container, which led investigators to the claimant's drug laboratory, had been equipped with a transmitter while still in the store and with the consent of the store's owner. No one, after all, could expect the constitutional right to privacy while travelling on public streets. In Knotts's case, however, no consideration was given to the question of whether the use of a tracking device in someone's private home might represent a violation of the Fourth Amendment.

This matter would have to be evaluated by the Supreme Court a year later. In their efforts to follow James Karo, investigators planted a tracking device on a container of ether and sold it through informants to the suspect. By following the locational information from Karo's apartment to his drug laboratory, they were ultimately able to arrest him. In this case, the judges reached a different decision; they regarded the tracking of radio signals from within the suspect's home to be a search in the constitutional sense and thus as a procedure requiring a warrant. As in Katz's case, it was determined that there is no difference between entering a private space physically and doing so with a transmitter. The plaintiff was thus vindicated in this regard, but his sentence was nevertheless upheld on account of all the other evidence against him.

These two rulings established the basic legal principle that has since governed police use of location technology in the United States – namely, that it is permissible to locate a suspect by such means so long as the acquisition of such information is restricted to public space. A tracking device that is planted in a container of chloroform and traced for a few hours on the road does not represent an unreasonable search; in contrast, a tracking device smuggled into someone's private residence does. In the mid-1980s, however, a suspect's vehicle remained a sort of grey zone: "The Supreme Court," as John Hall noted at the time in an article about the legal status of tracking devices, "has not yet decided whether the installation of a beeper in or on a vehicle constitutes a fourth amendment search."[20] Yet, with the arrival of GPS technology, which simplified and expanded geographic surveillance, this became a standard practice of law enforcement. Now it is no longer necessary for a patrol car to be in the vicinity of a suspect in order to receive a signal from a beeper every 30 seconds. Instead, a GPS transmitter the size and weight of a credit card is simply planted on a suspect's vehicle, and detectives receive continuous tracking information on their cell phones.

At the end of a long legal battle in the United States, which took place from 2003 to 2013, the Supreme Court had to evaluate the legality of this practice as well. In this case, a convicted producer of cocaine (a nightclub owner named Antoine Jones) had been sentenced to life in prison because the locational data sent from a GPS transmitter on the bottom of his Jeep, which amounted to around 2,000 pages of printed evidence, irrefutably proved his criminal activity. Although the detectives behind this arrest did receive a warrant to plant the transmitter, it was only valid for ten days and within the city limits of Washington, DC. The actual act of surveillance, however, lasted considerably longer (it ended four weeks after the deadline) and was also conducted throughout the entire state of Maryland. In early 2012, the Supreme Court judges decided that the GPS-aided acquisition of data in this case represented a search under the Fourth Amendment and was thus unconstitutional. The case was then remanded to the district court; in a subsequent trial held the following year, which relied on different sorts of evidence, Jones was sentenced (almost a decade after the initial investigations) to 15 years of prison with credit accorded for the time he had already served.

The rulings in *United States* v. *Jones* vividly expose the dynamics and conflicts that universally available GPS technology has engendered in digital culture. By the end of 2011, when the Supreme Court first heard the case, location services were already a ubiquitous reality on smartphones. The judges of course took this into account, and they repeatedly juxtaposed the two divergent applications of the system – its use by the police and its use in everyday communication. Although a unanimous decision was reached about the FBI's delayed installation of the tracking device and the inordinately long period of surveillance, the nine judges were so divided regarding the fundamental reasons for this conclusion that three different opinions were written about the use of location technology in police investigations. The degree of rigor with which the respective judges opposed the new tracking technology depended on the varying extents to which they still adhered to the constitutional text from 1791. Thus, their opinions reflected the precarious relationship between the permanence of the law and the impermanence of modern media landscapes.

One group of four judges, who in 2012 had advocated a categorical ban on warrantless GPS surveillance, argued in terms of a rather ahistorical and orthodox understanding of the law that deferred to the original language of the Fourth Amendment (even despite the eighteenth-century context of its composition). Their stated objective was to apply, in the twenty-first century, "an 18th-century guarantee against unreasonable searches."[21] In contrast, a second group of four judges (and Judge Sotomayor, who wrote her own opinion) focused on the obsolete qualities of the Fourth Amendment and argued that the historical context of the Constitution ought to be taken into account. Legal categories such as the "unreasonable search," they claimed, should be evaluated in light of the "dramatic technological change" that has recently led to "significant changes in popular attitudes."[22] Technical devices and applications that enable the monitoring of a person's movements, according to this faction of the Court, "may provide increased convenience or security at the expense of privacy, and many people may find the tradeoff worthwhile."[23] Samuel Alito, who authored the opinion on behalf of the group, singled out the location services on cell phones as one of the most significant recent developments: "[C]ell phones and other wireless devices now permit wireless carriers to track and record the location of users – and as of June 2011, it has been reported, there were more than 322 million wireless devices in use in the United States."[24] "The availability and use of these and other new devices," Alito continued, "will continue to shape the average person's expectations about the privacy of his or her daily movements."[25] In an oral argument made a few weeks before the final decision, Alito expressed in concrete terms what he thought such changes might entail: "Suppose we look forward 10 years, and maybe 10 years from now 90 percent of the population will be using social networking sites, and they will have on average 500 friends, and they will have allowed their friends to monitor their location 24 hours a day, 365 days a year, through the use of their cell phones.... What would the expectation of privacy be then?"[26] And it was precisely this trend in digital culture's approach to locational data that led his faction to argue in favor of the flexible and short-term use of GPS surveillance in future criminal investigations, even without a warrant. Under such conditions, Alito concluded, "relatively short-term monitoring of a person's movements on public streets accords with expectations of privacy that our society has recognized as reasonable."[27]

This is a statement with far-reaching implications: investigators should be permitted to make use of short-term GPS tracking simply because the process has become culturally assimilated through the everyday use of digital communication. By the year 2001, that is, aspects of police surveillance that were at risk of violating personal rights had already been put into wide practice through the voluntary use of location services on cell phones. Sonia Sotomayor, who wrote her own opinion, concurred with the Court's recommendation to ban the use of GPS tracking without a warrant, but her reasoning concerned the abundance of information – "a wealth of details about [a person's] familial, political, professional, religious, and sexual associations" – that surveillance of this sort could reveal about someone: "Disclosed in [GPS] data ... will be trips the indisputably private nature of which takes little imagination to conjure: trips to the psychiatrist, the plastic surgeon, the abortion clinic, the AIDS treatment center, the strip club, the criminal defense attorney, the by-the-hour motel, the union meeting, the mosque, synagogue or church, the gay bar and on and on."[28] On the one hand, this colorful list sheds some light on Judge Sotomayor's conception of secretive and potentially shameful milieus; on the other hand, it immediately calls to mind the function of the "frequent locations" application on the iPhone 5s. As mentioned above, this service records all of the places where the user has been over the past six weeks and ranks them according to the frequency and duration of the visits. Of course, this usually amounts to a collection of banal and predictable information: one's own apartment, the office, the neighborhood supermarket, and so on. It is a protocol of regular life. Yet this service also records all of the deviations from one's normal existence, such as, for instance, the recurring scene of a love affair. For a distrusting husband or wife, such lists of "frequent locations" would be a dependable source of information – just as reliable, in fact, as a GPS tracking device planted on the vehicle of someone running a drugs lab.

The Supreme Court's ruling in the case against Antoine Jones had immediate effects on the FBI's surveillance standards, and Robert Mueller, who was then the director of the agency, acknowledged as much just a few months after the announcement of the verdict. Of the nearly 3,000 ongoing cases in which GPS surveillance was being used by American police, several hundred were required to adopt new tracking methods after the Court's decision.[29] Thus, despite the ubiquity of location services on smartphones, it has since been illegal in the United States for the police to track someone's location with this technology unless certain conditions apply and a warrant has been procured. In Germany, the issue incited a similarly protracted legal dispute, but its resolution was entirely different. There, a lawsuit filed in 1996 by a member of the "Anti-Imperialist Cell" – whose vehicle had been tracked with GPS surveillance and who had consequently been sentenced to 13 years in prison for setting off explosives – was finally rejected nearly 10 years later. The issue debated by the Federal Constitutional Court was whether the installment of a GPS transmitter on the suspect's vehicle was in accordance with section 100c of the *Criminal Procedure Code*, an article ratified in 1992. At the time of the arrest, this section stipulated the following: "[T]echnical means intended for the purposes of surveillance may be used to establish the facts of the case or to determine the whereabouts of the perpetrator provided the investigation concerns a criminal offense of considerable importance."[30] In their ruling on the case, the judges concluded that the use of GPS technology was covered by the provisions of the law: "Interventions in the general right of personality by means of technical instruments of observation typically do not, in their scope and intensity, breach the inviolable core of private life. So it is in this case as well."[31] In 2010, this ruling was upheld by the European Court of Human Rights.

Debates over the use of GPS in criminal investigations have thus been defined by problems of legitimation. Even in the German case, which, unlike the later American proceedings, was decided in favor of law enforcement, the scope and complexity of the ruling demonstrated how varied and flexible the legal views of tracking procedures have to be. According to a decision reached by Germany's Federal Court of Justice in 2013, which prohibited private detectives from monitoring suspects with GPS surveillance, only executive authorities of the state are permitted to track suspected criminals by such means.[32] Who, then, has the legitimate right to determine another person's geographical location? And under what conditions is this allowed to happen? By this point, digital culture's everyday forms of communication have caused the heated legal battles over such questions of "authorization" to cool down entirely. Anyone who uses a smartphone with location services has already granted this authority by tapping the touchscreen and permitting the device to "share my location."

Electronic ankle bracelets

Before the end of the twentieth century, the act of locating individuals was restricted to exceptional situations of law enforcement; as mentioned above, it thus had another significant application in addition to its use in tracking suspects: the surveillance of already-convicted criminals by means of an apparatus that has come to be known as an "electronic ankle bracelet." The origins of this practice go even further back than the first uses of tracking devices in police manhunts and derive from the collaborative efforts of psychologists and criminologists. In the mid-1960s, Ralph Schwitzgebel, a student of the behaviorist B. F. Skinner at Harvard, began to take an interest in designing "behavioral electronics" – that is, in creating transmitters that could be attached to the body of a subject and would send continuous information about the latter's movements and impulses to a control laboratory. Among other things, Schwitzgebel imagined devices with which addicts or repeat offenders could convey their every thought about drugs or committing crimes by pushing a button on the transmitter, in order to provide the laboratory with real-time information about the dynamics of their inner lives. According to Schwitzgebel, the first stage would be to use the devices simply to observe the patients and delinquents in their usual environments. Ultimately, however, they could serve as a means of direct behavioral control by, for instance, "restricting voluntary actions or by eliciting involuntary ones."[33] His research soon led to a process that no longer involved the psychological interpretation of recorded signals – rather, it enabled him simply to monitor the location of his test subjects. In 1969, Schwitzgebel was granted a patent for an invention called the "Behavioral Supervision System with Wrist-Carried Transceiver." According to the patent application, the system could convey the position of its wearer every 30 seconds through a radio signal and was intended to be used for the surveillance of "selected individuals" – primarily criminals released on parole.[34]

Under the technological conditions of the time – and Schwitzgebel repeatedly stressed this himself – his device could only be regarded as a preliminary model. The transmitter and the battery, which the supervised individual was supposed to wear around his wrist, would have weighed nearly a kilogram; the mobile receiver units, which would transmit the signal to the central control station, had a range of just a few dozen meters, and so a great many of them would have to be installed just to monitor a subject's movement within a single city block. In 1969, Schwitzgebel conducted a series of experiments with 16 volunteers – "from an offender with over a hundred arrests and eight years of imprisonment, to a young business man with no criminal record" – and concluded that the range of the system was still quite limited, "covering only five or six blocks during street use and the inside of one large building."[35] In the history of the electronic ankle bracelet, Schwitzgebel's device is therefore little more than an uneventful prologue, and in fact it was all but forgotten by the early 1970s. Regarding the genealogy of certain conceptions of humanity in digital culture, however, it is significant that the location technology was first implemented to track individual people and, like the historical development of the profile, that it was based on a contribution of applied psychology to the field of law enforcement. The aim of this contribution, moreover, was to control and correct the behavior of unstable or deviant individuals by technical means: The term used by Schwitzgebel to promote the adoption of his electronic rehabilitation system – in both psychiatric and criminological settings – was "behavior modification."[36] Schwitzgebel repeatedly stressed the humanistic impulse behind his work. At a time when American prisons were dramatically overcrowded and experts were beginning to rethink the penal system, he thought his devices might pave the way for prisons to become "museums of our past inhumanity."[37] Yet this humanistic streak was tied to normative behavioral psychology's need to have relentless access to its subjects. As Foucault realized, moreover, the alleged ethical justifications for penal reforms typically turn out to be agendas for increasing efficiency. "When specific offending behaviors can be accurately predicted and/or controlled within the offender's own environment," or so Schwitzgebel and his colleagues fantasized in 1964, "incarceration will no longer be necessary as a means of controlling behavior and protecting society."[38]

In the late 1970s, the idea of electronically monitoring parolees was raised yet again, and this time it led to a state-sanctioned practice of law enforcement. These developments were apparently motivated by a comic strip. Jack Love, a district court judge in Albuquerque, has himself related the story of how, in the summer of 1977, a short *Spider-Man* comic in a newspaper had inspired his concept for automatically tracking convicted criminals. In the comic strip, the villain known as Kingpin attaches an unremovable location transmitter around the superhero's wrist: "That oversized I.D. bracelet," Kingpin explains triumphantly, "is an electronic *radar device* which will allow me to *zero in* on your location whenever I wish! Even your awesome *power* cannot remove it! *Nothing* can – except my hidden *laser key!*"[39] Reading this, Love thought that, if the relationship between the good guy and the bad guy were inverted, then such an

The *Spider-Man* comic from 1977 that supposedly inspired a judge in New Mexico to design the first electronic ankle bracelet.

"I.D. bracelet" might in fact be a useful way for the penal system to monitor and control criminals without having to rely on overcrowded prisons. At the time, the judge was obviously unfamiliar with Schwitzgebel's experiments in "behavioral electronics," which had been conducted a decade earlier. Yet, because Love's vision was not to monitor entire city districts but rather to introduce something like an electronically optimized version of "house arrest," his surveillance method could be realized far more easily and practically.

Inspired by the comic, and further driven by a fatal inmate riot in a nearby prison, Jack Love strove in subsequent years to implement this alternative model of sentencing. According to his own accounts, he struggled for a long time to convince a large computer company to develop models of the device. One of the firm's employees, however, eventually began to design radio transmitters the size of a pack of cigarettes, and with this product in mind he founded an independent company called NIMCOS ("National Incarceration Monitor and Control Services"). In 1983, Love attached a transmitter to his lower leg and conducted a three-week experiment on himself in order to test the reliability of the signal; in April of the same year, soon after the measure had received authorization from New Mexico's courts, he sentenced the first offender – a 30-year-old man who had broken the conditions of his parole – to a four-week period of electronically monitored house arrest. Over the following months, five probation violators in Albuquerque were sentenced to this form of confinement before technical difficulties and financial problems brought an end to the experiment. Around the same time, however, the city of Palm Beach in Florida began a similar attempt to convert short prison sentences or the remainder of certain sentences into periods of house arrest with electronic surveillance. Legal historians tend to consider this measure to be the first "fully functioning" example of location tracking in the history of the penal system,[40] and its implementation in Florida was so successful that the practice quickly spread elsewhere. By 1988, the "electronic ankle bracelet" had already been introduced in 33 US states; in Europe, the first experiments with such a system were conducted the following year in Great Britain, and Sweden began to look into the matter five years after that.

During the early stages of monitoring convicted criminals, the area of surveillance was limited to the perpetrators' homes. The prevailing system used at the end of the 1980s transmitted signals from a rather heavy ankle or wrist bracelet to a receiver in a phone jack, which in turn relayed information to a computer at the nearest correctional facility.[41] The range of the signal was about 60 meters. With the arrival of GPS technology in the mid-1990s, and especially with the strengthening of its civilian signal in the year 2000, the potential applications of the system multiplied. By now, a small transmitter attached to the body of an offender could track his or her exact position just about anywhere on earth. Ralph Schwitzgebel's dream has thus come true. Under today's conditions, the process of tracking offenders can be tailored to specific cases and to highly specific restraining orders – it is no longer a problem, for instance, to keep a close eye on a convicted stalker who is not permitted near his former victim's house, or to monitor an exhibitionist who has been banned from schools and parks.

In Germany, the concept of "electronic residential surveillance," as the practice is officially known, was first discussed at legal conferences at the beginning of the 1990s. Influenced by the results of pilot projects throughout Europe, the German Federal Council established a working group in 1997 devoted to "electronically monitored house arrest." In its final report, the group recommended this sort of confinement as a possible substitute for short-term prison sentences of one to six months. Yet the proposed legislation, which was debated in parliament in 1999, was never adopted (in 2006, incidentally, the federal government transferred the responsibility for penitentiary law to the individual German states). In 2000, Hessen nevertheless became the first state to introduce the method as a means of avoiding pretrial detentions and curtailing lengthy prison sentences. According to the legislators, this would make it easier for authorities "to monitor whether a convict was adhering to instructions to remain inside or leave his or her apartment at appointed times in order to grow accustomed to a regular daily routine."[42] Around 70 delinquents in Hessen were tracked in this way per year, bringing the total to 709 by 2010. For several years, as these numbers suggest, the electronic monitoring of parolees had not been an especially common practice in the German penal system.

Around this time, however, a ruling by the European Court of Human Rights opened up a new area of application for GPS technology, and this led to a steep increase in the number of delinquents being monitored in such a way. In 2009, the Strasbourg-based Court declared that any preventive detention lasting more than ten years after the end of a prison sentence was inhumane, and this caused the judicial apparatus in Germany and other countries to be confronted on a daily basis with the question of how to go on controlling the behavior of a throng of suddenly released inmates. With unusual speed, a new paragraph was therefore added to the Criminal Code to "reform the law on preventive detention," and it went into effect at the beginning of 2011. This new ordinance, according to one of the judges involved, "was guided by the effort to reconfigure in a more efficient manner the instrumentation for monitoring former parolees now living in freedom."[43] One of the "auxiliary provisions" embedded in the law concerns the automatic tracking of individuals whose completed sentence or mandatory term of psychiatric treatment was at least three years behind them; a person with this status could now be instructed "to carry the equipment for the electronic monitoring of his whereabouts in working order with him at all times and not to tamper with them."[44]

In a critical essay from the year 2000 on the surveillance methods adopted in Hessen, Detlef Nogala and Rita Haverkamp remarked: "In principle, the only thing missing is the cell phone designed to function like one of these electronic bracelets."[45] One could say that this ironic prediction has come true, though not as yet another step toward the authoritarian surveillance regime imagined by the authors. Although it goes without saying that today's smartphone is an omnipresent tracking device that records its user's every movement in space, its logic is entirely different from that of the electronic ankle bracelet. It is not a sanctioning mechanism imposed by state or police authorities, but rather a freely available vehicle of self-empowerment. This ambivalent relationship is especially striking in the form of the recently released "Apple Watch." Since Schwitzgebel's time, transmitters for locating delinquents have just as often been meant to be worn around the wrist as around the ankle, and a comparison between the design of the wristbands used by the justice system and that of the Apple Watch reveals surprising similarities. It is not without reason, then, that bureaucratic descriptions of such control transmitters have repeatedly mentioned wristwatches as a point of reference: "Electronic surveillance," according to a commentary on the legislation enacted in 2011, "is typically discussed in the media in the same breath as 'electronic ankle bracelets.' This designation, however, is misleading. In its current form ratified by legislators, the instrument no longer has much in common with a fetter. The subject is not fettered to anything. He is rather mandated by the court to wear a device that resembles a (somewhat large) wristwatch and to ensure that it remains attached to his body and in working condition."[46]

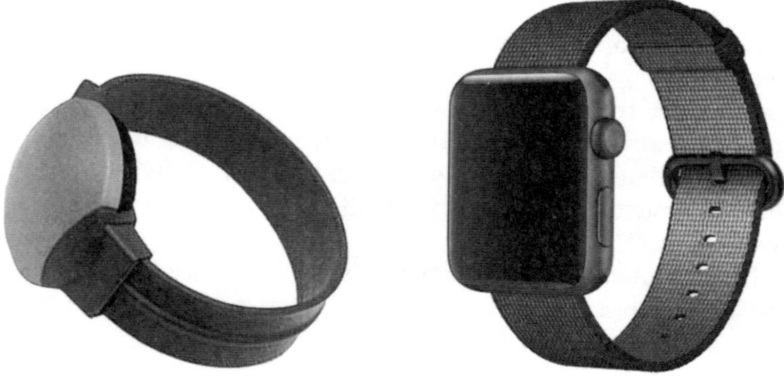

On the left, a device for electronically monitoring criminals (2009); on the right, the Apple Watch 1 (2015).

And so there are two different devices that are equipped with GPS technology and meant to be worn around the wrist: one a medium of control used by the justice system and criticized for potentially stigmatizing its wearer by visibly signaling his or her status under the law; the other, a sought-after status symbol whose store debut in April of 2015 enticed hundreds of buyers in New York, London, and Tokyo to wait in line overnight for the opportunity to spend the equivalent of 400 euros on it. Of course, the differences are considerable between a state-mandated surveillance wristband, which was at first intended to confine its wearer in his or her apartment, and a voluntarily acquired communication device that can be used without restrictions. In purely technical terms, the difference lies in the fact that the location services on a smartphone or smart watch only receive data (the users themselves have to give permission for their locations to be disclosed), whereas the device used for tracking convicts both transmits and receives. Nevertheless, it still needs to be asked what the collective desire for self-surveillance and self-locating over the past decade has meant for the status of the subject in the present day. The horrifying vision from 2010 of a cell phone functioning like an electronic ankle bracelet is today's banal reality, but this "fetter" is not perceived to be coercive and restrictive – rather, it is seen as liberating, social, and identity-shaping. The clearest argument for the distinctness of these two apparatuses is that delinquents are forced to use the transmitters while the owners of smartphones use location functions willingly. Yet this difference is not as sharp and categorical as it might seem at first glance; the two extremes tend to come together. Over the last 30 years, on the one hand, nearly every American and European device for monitoring locations has required the consent of the subject as a precondition for use (one of the most often cited efficiencies of this punitive measure is that, unlike a prison sentence, it also has to be *desired* by the delinquent in question).[47] On the other hand, the ostensibly voluntary nature of people locating themselves on their smartphones has to be weighed against the fact that the full effects of certain location functions – such as the "frequent locations" service mentioned above – are buried deep within the operating system and are thus invisible during everyday use. Not only does it take a degree of effort to turn off the location functions on a cell phone – by doing so, users are then excluded from so many universally established infrastructures. The voluntary and necessary aspects of locating oneself are thus constantly merging together.

The objective of Ralph Schwitzgebel's device from the 1960s was to "correct" the behavior of criminals and the mentally ill. More than 50 years later, this intention is still at the heart of the punitive implementation of electronic surveillance. In the case of those released on parole, a transmitter worn around the arm or leg remains, according to lawmakers, "the only suitable means of controlling behavior."[48] What does this category imply, however, about digital culture's fervid passion for self-location? What sorts of "behavioral control" arise from the internal services and uploaded applications on smartphones and smart watches – services and applications that determine and convey the locations of their users a dozen times per day? Given the strict legal requirements that limit the electronic surveillance of convicted criminals, the intensity with which people are tracked in everyday communication is far higher. According to the German "Act to Reform the Law on Preventative Detention," for instance, the home of the subject on probation is "fundamentally excluded from surveillance as a space exempt from monitoring."[49] This limitation is meant to ensure that the practice of long-term surveillance conforms with basic rights such as the "right to informational self-determination." While a delinquent is at home, the penal system is forbidden from creating a detailed profile of his or her movements; in this situation, the surveillance is reduced to the information that he or she is simply present on the premises. In legal discussions of this punitive measure, the question is often raised of whether the initial installation of a transmitter in the home of the monitored might itself constitute a violation of personal rights.

In legal terms, the court-mandated surveillance of criminals is thus far less "intrusive" than the act of locating oneself on a smartphone. It is characteristic of today's ambivalent disposition, moreover, that the dystopia of total surveillance – a source of dread up until the end of the twentieth century – seems to have been realized and yet not realized at the same time. In an essay published in 1988, the criminologist Thomas Feltes envisioned a "futuristic scenario" of "criminality and control in the twenty-first century," in which he attempted to imagine future punitive practices "in light of current developments" such as electronic surveillance. As with all science fiction, his visions of the future say more about the time that they were conceived than anything else. Although Feltes had a good sense of the technical changes to come – "the transmitter worn around the ankle or wrist will become smaller and smaller, while its range will continue to expand" – the conditions of use that he foresees are really just amplifications of the collective fear of being recorded that pervaded the 1980s. The author's speculations advance from a small transmitter card, which has to be worn constantly by everyone for the sake of tracking and identification, to a computer chip implanted beneath the skin, "which, as a general means of control, will have to be replaced every ten years or so." The power relations are clear in all of this: individuals will be controlled by an unspecified state authority. The chip, according to Feltes, "can be programmed externally at will, and its storage capacity will be as good as unlimited."[50]

A product of its time, Feltes's political perspective concerning technically optimized control was fueled by contemporary debates about census-taking, machine-readable IDs, and the realization of Orwell's "big brother."[51] No criminologist from 30 years ago could have foreseen the present circumstances in which identification cards, transmitters, and chips operate as extensively and intensively as predicted and yet, rather than giving rise to totalitarianism, have instead engendered a free community of highly networked people who incessantly "share" their opinions, information, and locations. Feltes explained the imminent domination of technology in the year 2017 as the triumph of "post-modern nihilism," the seeds of which he detected in the "No Future" and "New Wave" movements of his time.[52] Nothing could be further from the social utopia of today's sharing culture – from the spellbound eavesdroppers fulfilling Mark Zuckerberg's bright-eyed vision or the enraptured young families browsing through Airbnb's website – than the world-renouncing punks of the 1980s.

Location-based games

The electronic surveillance of suspects and criminals, which began in the 1970s, thus represents the first major turning point in the use of location technology. What had once been employed exclusively by the military to track the locations of vehicles and weapons was now being applied by the police and the courts to monitor the locations of individual people.

Yet how did the next major change come about – namely, the development from locating deviant individuals to the omnipresent communication formats of digital culture? What technological, cultural, and mental shifts were needed to convert the constant tracking of individuals, which until recently had been a highly criticized practice permitted only under exceptional circumstances, into the basis of playful activities, business models, and romantic connections? As early as 1995, the year in which GPS became fully operational, a veteran engineer in the field was already sufficiently confident to make the following prediction: "Before long, everything that moves could have a GPS chip inside. By this I mean every telephone, every portable PC, every vehicle, every hiker."[53] At this time, the installation of mobile navigation systems in cars was already a blossoming business and, by the end of the 1990s, "the use of digital location technology took off on a mass scale."[54] Methods for determining the locations of individuals, however, were not yet a feature of cell phones, which were already in widespread use at the time. This synthesis of location and communication instruments did not take place until the early 2000s, and three developments were responsible for it: the mobile internet; the precise (even in urban environments) and undistorted transmission of GPS signals; and, a little later, the bundled services offered in app stores. It was this combination of factors that gave rise to the smartphone.

The decision to put an end to the artificial weakening of GPS signals had an almost immediate effect on the establishment of location services in digital culture. In May 2000, as mentioned above, the American government lifted this restriction on civilian use, and this led at once to a boom in the development of so-called location-based services. "It is not an overstatement," as the media historian Jordan Frith has noted in retrospect, "to say that if the U.S. government had maintained SA [Selective Availability], the types of locative media used today would not exist."[55] At first, however, the number of people who could make use this of service was still minimal; in the years just after 2002, when web-enabled cell phones were still largely associated with the BlackBerry brand, the devices were regarded more or less as status symbols for business people. This situation changed radically as of 2007. In late June of that year, Apple brought out the first iPhone; in October 2008, moreover, the first smartphone equipped with Google's Android operating system became available, along with a corresponding platform for software applications known as the Android Market (today's Google Play). Running on the data-processing standard called 3G, these apparatuses quickly transformed the smartphone into an everyday object. By the end of 2008, nearly a third of all Europeans possessed such a device.[56]

Location services have been part of the package from the beginning. With Apple's Loopt application and the service known as Latitude, which is integrated with Google Maps, smartphone users were now able to share their locations at any moment with a select circle of acquaintances. "Staying in touch with friends can be tough," as we were told in an early iPhone advertisement from 2008, "but if you have Loopt from the App Store, you know what they're up to, where they are, and if they want to grab lunch." Self-locating thus began to establish itself as a communication format of digital culture. The year 2009 saw the launch of Foursquare, a location-based service that boasts around 45 million registered users today. Part location service and part social network, the app encourages its users to "check in" with their smartphones when arriving at bars, cafés, or restaurants in order to make it easier to meet acquaintances during a busy night out and to earn rewards for visiting certain establishments frequently.

Like the development of the profile format described in the previous chapter, this new fondness for self-locating (along with the simultaneous rise of social networks) conflicted with some of the foundational fantasies of the internet as a medium. In his 1995 manifesto *Being Digital*, for instance, Nicholas Negroponte made the following prediction: "We will socialize in digital neighborhoods in which physical space will be irrelevant."[57] A precondition for these imagined utopias of freedom was of course the "placelessness" of online communication – an internet user's physical location is irrelevant when he or she is moving around in cyberspace. It is precisely this emancipation from ascribed identities and positions that came to an abrupt end with the arrival of social media and smartphones. This transition, which is associated with the advent of the so-called "Web 2.0" (a term introduced in 2004), meant above all that users now had to have fixed identities and positions: a "profile" and a "location." The much-vaunted rise of the "social" as the internet's new disposition is thus synonymous with the medium's adoption of tracking methods used by the police. In becoming the "Web 2.0," the medium of the internet thus underwent a process of devirtualization.

One social practice that has benefitted considerably from this fundamental change is the game. Since the turn of the twenty-first century, so-called "geocaching," a scavenger hunt directed by electronic location media, has been one of the most popular applications of GPS technology for private citizens. Smartphone services such as Foursquare, too, owe much of their popularity to the fact that they have turned the mere act of locating other users into a friendly competition.[58] The changed status of tracked or located individuals – from victims to autonomous agents, from deviants to respectable citizens – thus took place in the mode of play. The Foursquare app is an excellent example of the process in digital culture that is referred to as "gamification," which denotes the conversion of rather serious and unplayful interests – such as the business model of earning money from other people's locational data – into ludic practices.

Aside from *Pokémon Go*, which briefly took the world by storm, the most interesting manifestation of this phenomenon is undoubtedly *Ingress*, a location-based and augmented-reality game that was first introduced in 2012 and has been available on smartphones since 2014. By this point it had attracted millions of players, who typically gathered at centrally organized meetings in large American, European, or Asian cities to participate on a mass scale. *Ingress*'s playing field is the entire world, in the form of a futuristically distorted version of Google Maps; it is activated by downloading an app and agreeing to be located throughout the duration of the game. The opening display reads as follows: "*Ingress* is a location-based game. Your location is collected by this application and may be visible to other users as you take certain actions in the game." The back story of the game is that a secret organization has covered the world with a mysterious form of mind-hacking energy that is concentrated in particular places known as "portals." These portals are real buildings, monuments, businesses, cafés, and kiosks; any *Ingress* player can suggest new portals by sending pictures to the company for them to be considered and registered. The large crowd of players is divided into two factions: the "Enlightened," who want to profit from the energy, and the "Resistance," who attempt to fight them off. When signing up, a player has to decide which side to be on. The objective of the game is to rove around the streets with a smartphone to discover such a portal (in Berlin, there is such a high number of players that there seems to be a portal on every corner), take control of it with the help of other players on one's team, and ultimately connect it with two other portals to form a triangle in space (the triangle can extend across a street, city, country, or even over an ocean). There are apparently many people who now plan their vacations around the possibility of coordinating with players on different continents, with whom one can remain in constant contact through the *Ingress* app, in order to create the largest possible triangle for one's faction, thereby gaining dominion over all of the strange energy within it.

Regardless of how fascinating or bizarre this mixture of geocaching and fantasy role-playing might seem, what is interesting about *Ingress* and its millions of worldwide portals is the novel relationship that has been created between the fictionality of the game's narrative and the reality of the space in which the game is played. From a technical perspective, what is staged as a paranoid fantasy – strange forms of energy covering the earth, "inspiration particles" that have to be collected[59] – is essentially just an opportunity for the parent company, Niantic Games (a subsidiary of Google), to collect detailed information about the locations and routines of millions of users. "A game extends only as far as its platform, its console. … But this is more than a game," a distorted voice intones at the beginning of play, underscoring the intensity of the challenges that lie ahead, and in a certain sense this statement is exactly right. *Ingress* may indeed be an entertaining and even addictive game that accompanies its players wherever they might go, all the while providing a more appealing and exciting dual reality. As a prime example of gamification, however, it is also a powerful vehicle for recording and controlling the movements of its users. In 2014, for instance, Niantic Games partnered with the telecommunications company Vodafone and, at least for a while, transformed all of the latter's stores and kiosks into portals. Here one cannot help but think of Ralph Schwitzgebel and his "behavioral electronics," which this concept seemed to have revived to great effect: by means of a playfully organized steering mechanism, innumerable potential customers were coaxed to walk on their own two feet to prescribed destinations in order to fulfill a company's marketing goals.

This constant and comprehensive tracking, however, also leaves detectable traces in space that can be followed by the participants. Although the smartphone screen, which shows every *Ingress* player a radius of up to 500 meters around his or her location, does not indicate within this radius the location of other players, their presence can be indirectly revealed through a continuously updated ticker at the bottom of the display, which indicates nearby activity and is reconfigured in the form of maps on fan sites devoted to the game. A player can thus stay informed about which usernames control which portals in the vicinity and can reconstruct, with a minimal amount of deductive effort, the preferred routes, frequently visited locations, and thus the actual homes and workplaces, of these people. For, beneath *Ingress*'s shimmering fantasy world, there is an actual city map. Within a given neighborhood, a regular user can track the movements of fellow players in their totality. It does not take much to imagine the sorts of situations that this could lead to. Is it outlandish to think, for instance, that a burglar who is familiar with augmented-reality games might spy on certain *Ingress* players in the neighborhood simply to learn exactly when and for how long they are out of the house?

Like the location services described at the beginning of this chapter, the accurately mapped-out cosmos of *Ingress* offers an inexhaustible source of *suspicion*. Yet perhaps, in digital culture, this very association or notion is evidence of traditional logic and an outmoded paradigm of epistemological constellations in which every clue leads to a case and every detail points to a broader context. In a recent work, the sociologist Luc Boltanski analyzed the sciences and narratives of suspicion in their heyday – namely, in the decades around 1900. These years gave rise almost at the same time to the psychiatric diagnosis of paranoia and the literary genre of the spy novel – two models in which things are not as they initially seem and in which mysteries and conspiracies can conceal (until uncovered by the efforts of an analyst or a detective) a more genuine world lurking beneath the veil of visible reality. Around the turn of the twentieth century, according to Boltanski, "generalized suspicion" constituted a "mental outlook": a constellation that also applied to the newly established scientific fields of sociology, criminology, and psychoanalysis, and that Carlo Ginzburg famously referred to as the "evidential paradigm."[60]

Yet how do the location technologies of digital communication relate to this understanding of the world? When the act of tracking people with transmitters and electronic ankle bracelets began to take shape in the 1980s and 1990s, its critics were still arguing according to these same categories and concepts: "Police access to mechanized control systems that, at first, existed and were operated beyond the purview of law enforcement," according to an article from 1995 about the new role of GPS in the field of criminology, threatens to give rise to "a society of generalized suspicion."[61] Today, such access is no longer limited to the police and the justice system – rather, smartphone producers, software developers, or game developers can access technology of this sort with unprecedented ease. The paradigm of suspicion is as close-knit as ever, but it is no longer a cause of apprehension for those caught in its mesh.

3

Cavity Searches: Bodily Measurements and the Quantified-Self Movement

The newfound desire to measure one's own bodily activity resulted from an awareness of human inadequacies. This, at least, is the starting point taken in the essay that first popularized the burgeoning practice of "self-tracking" in digital culture. In April 2010, the technology journalist Gary Wolf, who had founded the so-called "quantified-self movement" two years before, published an article in the *New York Times Magazine* that focuses on the divide between the objectivity of electronically collected bodily data and the inaccuracy of subjective forms of perception and expression. "[M]any of our problems," the author observes, "come from simply lacking the instruments to understand who we are. Our memories are poor; we're subject to a range of biases; we can focus our attention on only one or two things at a time.... We lack both the physical and the mental apparatus to take stock of ourselves." And from this sobering diagnosis he draws the following conclusion: "We need help from machines."[1]

In this much-discussed text, Wolf stresses that, whereas faith in the evidential value of numerical data is uncontested in scientific, economic, or political contexts, the "cozy confines of personal life" had long managed to remain untouched by this instrument of knowledge. Beyond keeping a journal, any form of detailed self-documentation seemed somewhat ridiculous, or even creepy. This attitude, according to Wolf, is currently undergoing a radical shift. In recent years, he has observed a "self-tracking explosion": "Sleep, exercise, sex, food, mood, location, alertness, productivity, even spiritual well-being are being tracked and measured, shared and displayed." The essay mentions a number of techniques used by "quantified-self" enthusiasts to do such things as count their every step, constantly record their blood pressure, track the hours and quality of their sleep, or painstakingly document changes in their mood. All together, these are people who, as Wolf remarks, would have been dismissed as oddballs not long ago but today are regarded as pioneers of a thriving movement. They are replacing the "vagaries of intuition with something more reliable," and they are dismissing what had formerly been considered an "inchoate flow of mental life" for the clearly differentiated, identifiable, and cross-referenced elements of a "quantified self." As for the reasons behind the growing popularity of self-tracking, Wolf cites four technological developments: smaller and more accurate electronic sensors; micro-computers in the form of smartphones; social media as a place for sharing one's findings; and the seemingly unlimited memory capacity of the "cloud." These four elements of digital culture have made it possible to collect data about one's own body and psyche – a formerly expensive procedure reserved for scientific and medical laboratories – simply by using a smartphone to unite a number of previously separate testimonies about one's identity: diary entries, bills of health, medical records, personal IDs, and so on.

The goal is to attain a better understanding of human beings through measurements, and Wolf places this approach in opposition to another technique, one that represented, throughout the twentieth century and beyond, the zenith of our ability to know anything about ourselves: "A hundred years ago," he reflects, "a bold researcher fascinated by the riddle of human personality might have grabbed onto new psychoanalytic concepts like repression and the unconscious. These ideas were invented by people who loved language. Even as therapeutic concepts of the self spread widely in simplified, easily accessible form," he goes on, "they retained something of the prolix, literary humanism of their inventors. From the languor of the analyst's couch to the chatty inquisitiveness of a self-help questionnaire, the dominant forms of self-exploration assume that the road to knowledge lies through words." Proponents of the quantified-self movement are taking "an alternate route": "Instead of interrogating their inner worlds through talking and writing, they are using numbers" – a dichotomy that the author also underscores by juxtaposing what might lie beneath the surface with what is simply on it. Wolf thus draws a sharp distinction between the goals and methods of self-measuring and those of therapeutic culture: "When we quantify ourselves," according to his essay, "there isn't the imperative to see through our daily existence into a truth buried at a deeper level. Instead, the self of our most trivial thoughts and actions, the self that, without technical help, we might barely notice or recall, is understood as the self we ought to get to know."

What Gary Wolf overlooks here – or intentionally fails to mention – is the fact that the preference for measurable data over mere words is of course not a radically "alternate route" of human understanding but rather a new rendition of an old anthropological debate. From their very beginning, the human sciences have wrestled with the question of whether it was best to interpret human beings through linguistic or bodily signs. In the history of knowledge about the self, Freud's "talking cure" did not, as Wolf would like us to believe, set in place a non-referential foundational paradigm; rather, the psychoanalytic method around the year 1900 should be understood as a prevalent stage within a long scientific dispute that first came to a head in the famous "physiognomy debate" between Johann Caspar Lavater and Georg Christoph Lichtenberg in the 1770s. In his aphorisms and disquisitions against the principles of physiognomy, Lichtenberg contested the idea that intellectual inclinations and personal characteristics could be deciphered from human facial features, but his insistence on the anthropological value of language ("Ten words from the language of a people are more valuable to me than one hundred of their speech organs preserved in alcohol"[2]) remained, within the newly founded human sciences and among their most prominent representatives, a marginal position throughout the entire nineteenth century. In contrast, Gall's phrenology, Broca's craniometry, Lombroso's criminal anthropology, Fechner and Wundt's psychophysics, or Galton and Bertillon's anthropometry cemented the belief in the objective measurability of human beings, their bodies, and their psyches. Processes of standardization, classification, and discrimination were validated on the basis of such measurable findings. And even when psychoanalysis established itself as an instrument of self-knowledge, it did not, as Wolf claims, occupy an exclusive or monopolistic position within this sphere of knowledge. Competing disciplines such as psychotechnics or (later on) behaviorism, which endeavored to evaluate the "inner man" on the basis of measurable data instead of words, exerted a similar amount of influence over the course of the twentieth century.

Not least for these reasons, it is instructive to examine the popularity of self-measuring techniques in today's digital culture, which for the past decade have been subsumed under umbrella terms such as "life-logging" or the "quantified self," in terms of their historical and scientific genealogy. Although the origin stories of their advocates tend to suggest otherwise, these movements did not arise from nothing. Without a doubt, their specific practices are due to the technological conditions of the last 15 years, but their basic approaches to acquiring knowledge can be traced back to far older scientific models. One of these models pertains to the conviction of self-trackers that there must be a consistently reliable – "natural," as it were – translational code between bodies and the data in question. The measurements are thought to speak for themselves, and the channels that translate the obscure and amorphous interiority of "bodily sensations" and "moods" into numbers and graphs are believed to be invulnerable to distortions, errors, and misreadings. Mechanically generated data have no history, no contingencies. This is the guiding belief of the quantified-self movement, just as it has been constitutive of the measuring principles followed by the human sciences since their beginnings.

The activity of self-tracking raises fundamental questions about the status of the subject in digital culture, questions that have also been addressed in my discussions of the profile concept and the widespread use of location technologies. Which aspects of these methods should be understood as emancipatory, and which should be understood as suppressive? In his essay, Wolf speaks about the ambition to "democratize" knowledge about our own bodies by means of smartphones and freely accessible, digital measuring instruments. Yet this attempt is opposed by another tendency or constellation, which Wolf himself mentions in passing. This is the "policeman inside all of our heads," who has been brought to life by the self-trackers' uncurbed desire to be recorded.[3] The question remains to what extent these two views of the self – one emancipatory, the other from the perspective of the police – supplement each other or come into conflict.

Fitbit

In his article, Wolf also mentions a young company from San Francisco that, in the fall of 2009, put a device on the market that can count the steps of its wearers, calculate the number of calories they have burned, and measure the quality of their sleep. At this time, the so-called "Fitbit" tracker still had the form of a clasp and was meant to be attached to a belt or pocket. It was not until 2013 that the company began to install the sensor in colorful plastic bracelets, which, together with the availability of its own smartphone app, drastically increased the sales of the device and turned it into a distinctive feature of the growing quantified-self movement. Today, Fitbit has a market value of around 6 billion dollars and has become the gold standard of the so-called "wearables" industry. In 2017, the company was responsible for a quarter of the more than 100 million wearable sensors sold worldwide.[4]

The assortment of Fitbit products now includes around ten models, from a simple clip to a digital scale. The company's most popular devices are currently its screenless "Flex" wristband, which can be purchased in Germany for 79 euros, and its "Charge" smart watch, which sells for 149 euros. In the Fitbit Flex, a motion sensor measures the total number of steps taken in a day in the form of flashing points (one point represents 2,000 steps, and five the daily target of 10,000). To monitor the quality of their sleep, which the wristband records by tracking a body's movement during the night, users have to activate the Fitbit app, which translates the tracker's findings into graphs and tables. This app is also needed to see how many calories have been burned throughout the day. The more expensive Charge model presents most of its measurements directly on the watch's screen. In addition to counting calories and steps, it can also measure one's heart rate and rank the activity required by various athletic activities. It is also able to track its wearer's location with GPS (in case someone wants to review his or her jogging route, for instance), but this information is only displayed on the user's synchronized smartphone.

What, exactly, makes Fitbit's products so attractive for so many millions of people? How do they function differently from earlier devices designed to measure and improve one's own health and fitness? On Fitbit's website and in the remarks of "quantified selfers," one particular argument in favor of wearables recurs again and again, which is that such wristbands and related products enable, for the first time ever, utterly exhaustive data sets to be collected. Mobile self-tracking devices are, as Gary Wolf stressed, "meant to be carried on the body at all times,"[5] and Fitbit's own website concentrates on this omnipresence as well: "Every moment matters and every bit makes a big impact. Because fitness is the sum of your life. That's the idea Fitbit was built on – that fitness is not just about gym time. It's all the time."[6] Whereas, in past decades, the ambition to lead a healthy life consisted of interspersing brief periods of physical activity into one's sluggish workaday existence – the morning jog, time at the gym, taking the stairs instead of the escalator – Fitbit now promises to translate such periodic attentiveness to one's well-being into an ongoing condition. The instrument attached to one's body simultaneously serves as a constant means of both control and motivation. According to one of the company's YouTube videos, "Fitness doesn't follow a formula. It's the sum of your life."[7] In 2014, Fitbit attempted to illustrate this claim with a global advertising campaign that involved the recitation of a long string of compound words, each of which ended in "-fit." By wearing the products, that is, the customer could not only become "racefit" or "hikefit" but also "lovefit," "kissfit," or "dadfit," and thus aspects of life such as love, intimacy, and parental responsibility were lumped in with more conventional components of a "healthy" lifestyle. Accordingly, the campaign's hashtag was #itsallfit. The company's goal is therefore to record, in the name of fitness, data about one's entire existence, in which there is no longer any distinction between work and family, body and soul, productivity and downtime, or even between being awake and being asleep. For, "When it comes to reaching your fitness goals," as the company claims, "steps are just the beginning. Fitbit tracks every part of your day – including activity, exercise, food, weight, and sleep – to help you find your fit."[8]

In all of this emphasis on the seamlessness of life, it is possible to see a technological constellation that has become characteristic of digital culture on account of the general use of smartphones and the comprehensive availability of wireless networks over the past decade. The ubiquity of networks is one of the most important topics in media theory today and, as a concept, its pervasiveness is especially clear in advertising campaigns and promotions for self-tracking devices. Wearing a Fitbit product is related to using a treadmill at the gym in the same way that today's constant access to wireless networks is related to "dialing up" to the internet during the era of modems and desktops. This omnipresence of networks, moreover, also marks the central difference between digital fitness wearables and previous methods and devices for measuring oneself, such as the bathroom scale. Although the latter, which has been around since the 1920s, may have forged a similar connection between data, bodies, and the desire for optimization – it, too, involves outsourcing one's self-assurance to a technical apparatus – the measurements that it produces are ephemeral and can only be viewed by the person standing on it.[9] Fitbit and other self-tracking instruments, in contrast, are not concerned with people measuring themselves in the privacy of their own homes, and they are also unconcerned with the obsessive commitment of professional athletes, who often train in solitude to achieve new records. They are rather meant to encourage social and technological interaction among their users; in the quantified-self movement, body-consciousness and communication are inextricably intertwined. Fitbit's commercials underscore this alliance in two ways. On the one hand, they hardly ever show anyone alone, but rather couples, families, or groups of friends and colleagues who get together to exercise, take a walk, or prepare a healthy meal. On the other hand, these short clips always draw attention to the fact that Fitbit's products, in addition to being measuring instruments, are also tools for communication that can display, for instance, incoming calls or texts received on one's synchronized smartphone. Even the basic "Flex" model fulfills this function by relaying signals through its five blinking points. "Stay connected with your friends while working out," says one of the company's commercials,[10] which regularly show people interrupting their workouts to pick up the phone.

That Fitbit places a high value on networking is also apparent from the way it is always encouraging users to "share" their own data. Recall that Gary Wolf counted the establishment of social networks among the four technological preconditions behind the success of the quantified-self movement. Fitbit confirms this idea by its concerted efforts to combine the processes of self-measurement and self-recording with the practice of promulgating and comparing information within a community. Under the heading "Motivation & Friends" on its websites, one reads: "Use Facebook and email to find and connect with Fitbit friends so you can send motivational messages, share stats, and cheer each other on."[11] The network that every Fitbit customer is supposed to be building is thus simultaneously social and competitive: "Stay encouraged to move more by using your steps to climb the leaderboard, or compete with friends and family in Fitbit Challenges," as the company recommends.[12] On the one hand, the community of Fitbit members is thus one of friends and family; on the other hand, however, it is also a community of competitors. "Fitbit tracks every part of your day," and it does so in the name of a playfully presented but perpetual competition.[13]

This blending of the social and the competitive is significant, however, because the digital methods of self-measurement have by now been embedded in contexts that extend beyond that of their limited use by individuals or groups of personal acquaintances. Such broader contexts include, most importantly, private and state-run insurance agencies, which now increasingly tie their fees, services, and discounts to information provided by their customers' self-tracking devices. At the present moment, the dual function of wearables could not be clearer to see. The rhetoric of the quantified-self movement is about self-empowerment and nothing else. Thanks to the ease and reliability with which we are now able to monitor our own bodily functions (or so the argument goes on many blogs and forums), it is largely possible to do away with the traditional healthcare apparatus – places such as medical practices, laboratories, and pharmacies, whose services are too expensive and whose level of care is insufficient. The paternalistic relationship between doctors and patients has been supplanted by emancipated self-trackers: "These new smartphone apps and tracking devices," according to the technology writer Richard MacManus, "were putting people in control of their day-to-day health data for the first time.... [W]e're moving into a world where we are taking responsibility for our own health, or at least for the measurement and regular monitoring of key health data."[14] This promise of autonomy, however, is supposed to spring from an ensemble of data that, as the advertisements for Fitbit and similar products make clear, derives entirely from permeable networks. "Self-Knowledge Through Numbers," which is the motto of the quantified-self movement, is thus meant to be achieved within a completely open and interconnected web of relations that can only contribute to the knowledge of the self-tracker by appropriating knowledge from others.

Unprecedented sovereignty awaits, but only at the price of making oneself as identifiable as possible, and the conception of humanity entailed by digital self-tracking oscillates between these two poles. This ambivalence is especially apparent in the latest innovations devised by the insurance industry, which are subsumed under the umbrella term "smart insurance." Since July 2016, the company Generali, which, with some 14 million clients, is the second-largest insurance firm in Germany, has offered a supplementary program called "Vitality," which can be purchased in conjunction with a life- or disability-insurance policy. The cost of annual premiums and the opportunity for rebates and special benefits are determined by the number of so-called "Vitality points" that the insured person has accumulated throughout the previous year. After signing a contract, new customers are obliged to take a health test on the company's website and to download the "Vitality app" on their smartphones, which in turn has to be synchronized with a fitness wristband. Every step and every athletic activity is tallied and added to one's Vitality account (as of fall 2017, it is also possible to earn additional points by buying healthy groceries in participating stores, which will keep track of scanned barcodes and relay this information to Generali). When a new client is deemed to have met all the criteria of the health test, he or she is awarded the base-level status of "bronze."[15] High daily step counts, visits to the gym (which, like affiliated grocery stores, records this information and passes it along to the insurance company), health-conscious purchases, and regular preventative medical check-ups all add to the number of points. "Gold" status is achieved at 30,000 points, at which stage the customer's premium is reduced by up to 11 percent; a 16 percent reduction results from achieving the "platinum" status, which is granted at 45,000 points. Moreover, Generali has partnered with a variety of companies, including Adidas, Expedia, and some department stores, that will grant discounts of up to 20 percent for "gold" members of the program, and up to 40 percent for "platinum" members. Points expire at the end of every contract year, but customers are allowed to retain the status that they have earned.

"Know your health," "Improve your health," and "Enjoy your rewards" are the three edicts of Generali's Vitality program, which is the first of its kind in continental Europe (similar programs have existed in Great Britain and the United States for somewhat longer). "The goal is to motivate our clients to lead healthy lives and to reward their progress in doing so. This will redefine insurance in Germany."[16] Even statutory health-insurance agencies in Germany are beginning to develop similar rewards programs.[17] This proclaimed redefinition of insurance involves, above all, gaining access to a previously unknown and constantly updated abundance of information about every client in order to learn details about his or her exercise routines, eating habits, and general state of health (a client's blood sugar and cholesterol levels, for instance, will be conveyed to the company after each preventative check-up). "Here, every step you take counts. And all of these should be kept track of as well," states the Vitality program's website in language that could have been taken from a Fitbit commercial. The difference, however, is that the playful competition depicted on Fitbit's website, with its virtual prizes and friendly contests, has been transplanted into the hard economic reality of life and disability insurance, where decisions are made about one's health benefits and premium payments.

The relentless quantification of fitness has thus been accompanied by a new form of individualization in the fields of health insurance and healthcare. "Vitality points" (and similar concepts such as the so-called "health score" devised by the Swiss company Dacadoo, which is used to measure the physical and mental conditions of clients on a constantly updated scale between 1 and 1,000) are intended to transform the complex matter of health into a precisely calculable value that is regulated by the individuals themselves, and whose fluctuations can be traced back, almost in real time, to clearly identifiable causes such as physical activity or nutrition.[18] All of this focus on self-empowerment is therefore intervening in some of the basic operations of social and healthcare policy, which have been effective for more than a century. The concept of the "welfare state," as developed in late-nineteenth-century Europe, is beginning to transform into a concept that could be called the "welfare self." In this way, the practices of the quantified-self movement and their applications in the insurance industry are fueling a tendency that sociologists such as Ulrich Bröckling and Thomas Lemke first described more than a decade ago – namely, a new understanding of health as a commodity for which individuals have to take their own responsibility.[19] Accordingly, sicknesses and impairments are viewed less as the negative effects of social constellations than as the result of personal negligence, a lack of "motivation," and the failure to seek "preventative care." (Breast or colon cancer, for instance, are no longer regarded first and foremost as strokes of fate – they rather raise the question of why the patient had let things advance so far.) In this light, it is interesting that the Vitality website contains a freely accessible survey that any visitor can fill out to check his or her "Vitality Age." The first pages of the test request information about body measurements, eating habits, and workout routines before then turning to issues of "mental wellbeing": "During the last thirty days, how often have you felt worthless or so depressed that nothing could cheer you up?"[20] The content of this survey makes it clear that, according to the logic of the insurance program, one's lifestyle, physical condition, and mental health form an inseparable unit that is defined by clear cause-and-effect relations. Those who have poor eating habits or exercise too infrequently not only jeopardize their blood pressure and cholesterol levels but also their courage to get on with life. Self-tracking devices enable one to create a seamless protocol of this sort of lifestyle, and the comprehensive and all-encompassing promise of self-recording is confirmed by the fact that no distinction at all is made between the physiological and psychological implications of the measurements in question.

Genealogies of self-tracking

Measuring human beings: according to the understanding of the quantified-self movement, the function of this is to promote the autonomous acquisition of knowledge about one's own state of health and to improve one's own well-being. Whereas "profiles" in digital culture enable people to present their own biographies, and GPS technologies enable people to locate themselves in space, the devices and methods of self-measurement are supposed to improve people's understanding of their own bodies. Yet in this third context, too, it is instructive to examine the history of these devices and methods. When and under what circumstances did people begin to measure the human body, both its rigid structures (such as bone structures and the shape of the skull) and its more inconspicuous physiological expressions (including heart rate, blood pressure, breathing, and sweating)? Who was doing the measuring and who was being measured? And what sort of significance was attributed to these measurements?

In the recent essays and books that have come out about the quantified-self culture, the authors usually start off by mentioning a few of the movement's "precursors" from previous centuries – rigorous self-observers such as Benjamin Franklin, whose diary is full of detailed behavioral plans, or the obese doctor from South Carolina named John Lining, who in 1740 kept a yearlong log documenting all of his meals, drinks, and excretions in relation to the outdoor and indoor temperature, the time of day, and the air pressure, in order to reach conclusions about his own metabolism. These protagonists are meant to situate today's self-tracking methods within a long tradition – "personal tracking is not new," as one study notes[21] – but they lead down a minor, if not false, genealogical trail.

While these may indeed be comparable examples of people paying close attention to their own bodies and keeping detailed records of their observations, the presumptions and goals of the self-examining diarists from the late seventeenth and eighteenth centuries differed in many respects from those of the people who use today's "wearables." For one thing, their activity was based on Calvinist and puritanical principles – a set of religious morals that has more or less disappeared as a driving motivation. Second, their self-measurements and recordings took place in private spaces – in their own homes and in their personal diaries – and they were only made publicly available in the form of scientific reports. Third, the knowledge of these measurers was therefore linked to the peculiarity of their situation, and this self-understanding could manifest itself either as extraordinary virtue (in Franklin's case) or in the awareness of one's own eccentricity or idiosyncrasy.

Such idiosyncrasy, however, is in complete opposition to the fervent desire for comparison, competition, and the creation of standard values that has defined the quantified-self movement from the beginning. In a TED talk delivered in 2011, Gary Wolf projected four adjectives onto the wall to illustrate the goals associated with this new measurement culture: "thin," "rich," "happy," "smart." The objective of self-tracking, he says, "is to make us better in every way: thin, rich, happy, smart," and these new devices and methods "will make it easier for us to conform to expert advice about optimal human existence."[22] The quantified-self movement is not concerned with observing unique individuality, but rather with collecting data sets that can be compared and related to standardized norms. And it is precisely for this reason that it is methodologically unproductive to portray, as so often happens, the history of self-tracking as a succession of individual people who happened to analyze and measure their own bodies over the past few centuries. This history began instead at the moment when standardized and systematically implemented techniques made it possible to record, compare, and interpret human bodily measurements. For a sound genealogical analysis, the question of who was taking these measurements – the person being measured or someone else – is of the utmost importance because the devices and methods of today's quantified-self culture derive from scientific disciplines in which the distinction between the measurer and the measured was especially sharp.

In various contexts of knowledge during the second half of the nineteenth century, clear efforts were made to come to certain conclusions about human beings – about their inner lives, their biological dispositions, their affiliations with certain groups, and their immutable identities – on the basis of exact quantifications. Several new apparatuses, recording techniques, and measuring procedures were developed to answer such grand questions about humanity – questions that had previously been addressed in rather speculative terms – with scientific precision. The methods developed at the time can be categorized into two main areas of knowledge. On the one hand, anthropological principles were established for classifying and hierarchizing large cohorts of people by means of measuring their bodies, as with Paul Broca's craniometry or Cesare Lombroso's criminal-anthropological notion of the "born criminal" in the 1860s. This approach to recording the human physique led 20 years later to Francis Galton's and Alphonse Bertillon's variations of anthropometry, which included reliable methods – such as fingerprinting, which is still in use today – for identifying repeat offenders. Around this same time, on the other hand, new physiological measuring techniques were developed that were meant to yield more accurate information about human bodily functions. The second half of the nineteenth century gave rise to apparatuses such as the sphygmograph and the kymograph, which measured blood pressure and heart rates; the pneumograph, which measured the force of chest movements during respiration; and the plethysmograph, which could measure the volume of blood contained in a given organ. Unlike the measurements taken by Broca, Lombroso, or Bertillon, these methods of quantification were not intended to determine the general physical structures of large groups of people but rather to capture the fleeting and dynamic bodily expressions of the individual.

Interest in these devices quickly spread from the field of somatic medicine to other disciplines. In the 1860s, a new science called "psychophysics" studied the ways in which mental phenomena reacted to precisely measured physical stimuli. In 1879, a professor at Leipzig named Wilhelm Wundt founded the first institute for experimental psychology and attempted, by means of equipment typically used in physical or medical laboratories, to gain insights into the operations of human consciousness. As Wundt's student Hugo Münsterberg once remarked, such questions had previously "seemed the exclusive region of the philosophizing psychologist."[23] It was believed that the inner lives of human beings – their feelings, longings, fantasies – could be detected in the graphs produced by heart-rate and blood-pressure plotters. Münsterberg himself, whose professorial career took him to the United States in the 1890s, is largely responsible for popularizing the methods and results of Wundt's experiments. In his laboratory at Harvard University, which according to his own account consisted of "twenty-seven rooms overspun with electric wires,"[24] he attempted to transfer his teacher's knowledge about the relationship between physical reactions and mental processes into practical contexts such as economics, pedagogy, and criminal justice. In its optimism about the potential of measurements, this version of applied experimental psychology, which Münsterberg and others referred to as "psychotechnics," calls to mind the rhetoric of today's quantified-self movement: "With electrodes and the galvanoscope," as he wrote in his 1914 work *Grundzüge der Psychotechnik*, "we are able to demonstrate how the activity of sweat glands depends on changes in a person's consciousness; with the sphygmograph and the pneumograph, we can establish the extent to which emotional fluctuations influence a person's pulse and breathing patterns."[25] Precisely calculated body currents were thus regarded as media for the production of truth, and so it can be said that, toward the end of the nineteenth century, the scientific foundation was laid upon which today's self-trackers – who deduce their fitness, mood, and normality from data collected by instruments – continue to stand.

Yet what is telling about this foundation is that, around the year 1900, measuring human beings primarily meant measuring deviants and outliers. Paul Broca's skull measurements and the conclusions drawn from them about the size of the brain served above all to legitimize the hypothesis that dark-skinned people, by their very physical nature, possessed a lower capacity for intelligence than whites. Cesare Lombroso's anthropological criminology, in turn, relied on the investigation of thousands of skulls from the cemeteries and prisons of Turin in order to prove that criminal behavior derives from atavistic abnormalities. In the words of Lombroso's German translator and proponent Hans Kurella: "Lombroso has rediscovered in criminals certain features in common with the skulls of Neanderthals: the pronounced development of the brow, the thickness of the cranium, and a prominent bulge in the occipital bone."[26] According to this understanding, criminals are "evolutionary throwbacks in our midst," whose biological condition ineluctably gives rise to their delinquent biographies.[27] In Lombroso's later studies and in the work of his many students, this basic assumption led to the development of a multi-branched system for classifying deviants, a system that identified nearly a dozen types of "born criminals" according to specific physical and behavioral abnormalities.[28]

Given that it was intended to be used by the police, Alphonse Bertillon's anthropometry was by definition a means of measuring deviant subjects. According to Bertillon, his new identification system was a reaction to the "empty hope" of accomplishing anything with the recently created police archive containing photographs of every convicted criminal in Europe's major cities. The 100,000-odd photographs that the Paris police force had collected by 1880, for instance, had long ceased to be sorted and classified in any systematic manner. Photographs, moreover, are unreliable pieces of information if the goal is to determine the identity of recidivist criminals, whose outward appearances change with time and can be intentionally altered. Bertillon overcame this shortcoming by taking around a dozen measurements of every suspected criminal in areas of the body that would remain unchanged over the course of an adult lifetime. Among other things, he measured the length of their forearms, the length of their middle and little fingers, the length and width of their skulls, the size of their feet, and the length of their arm spans. He then classified each of these measurements into three different categories: "large," "medium," and "small."[29] From these classifications, it was possible to generate for every delinquent a so-called "anthropometric signature." The latter provided such an accurate representation of the people in question that, beginning in the 1880s, the police forces in large European cities soon found it easier and easier to answer the question of whether a given suspect had in fact already committed a crime within their precincts. For, altogether, the data sets provided by the measured body parts were so distinctive that, according to Bertillon, "only twelve out of every sixty thousand people will share approximately the same measurements."[30] In place of the amorphous and seemingly untamable mass of criminal photographs, Bertillon created a tightly knit archive consisting of hundreds of filing compartments, each of which contained just a few ID cards. These, then, could be used in conjunction with traditional means (such as names and the photographs on file) to reveal the identity of wanted criminals. "The majority of repeat offenders," Bertillon predicted, "will give up the hope that their tricks to remain at large will continue to be effective."[31]

No genealogy of the quantified-self should fail to mention that the development of measuring techniques during the second half of the nineteenth century was inextricably linked to the endeavor of identifying criminals. As Manfred Schneider noted in his book about the relationship between modern autobiographies and the human sciences, "The question of identity is a question of identifying deviance,"[32] and this statement applies just as well to the efforts of craniometry, anthropometric criminology, and psychotechnics. Not without a degree of pride, Bertillon was able to conclude one of his lectures with the following remarks: "In a word, the main objective of this new method is to determine the personality of everyone on a firm basis – to secure for every individual a reliable, permanent, and unchanging individuality."[33] From this it can be gathered that the notion of "personality" at the end of the nineteenth century was synonymous with an ensemble of data that, having been derived from intensive observation, situated human beings within the limits of what is "normal" and "tolerable." In this respect, bodily measurements took on a meaning that was similar to that of the first pedagogical and psychological "profiles" from the beginning of the twentieth century.

In terms of epistemology, this method was legitimized by the fact that the anthropologists, criminologists, and psychophysicists proceeded from the belief that an indisputable relationship existed between external features and internal conditions – between physical degenerations and corresponding mental, spiritual, and moral anomalies. In the words of Marcel Krause, Broca and Lombroso presupposed that there was an "absolutely transparent representational relationship"[34] between the skull, the brain, and one's mental disposition (the field of phrenology had made this same presupposition in the early nineteenth century, though its approach was speculative and did not rely on exact measurements), and Münsterberg's experiments likewise associated every rise in blood pressure and every acceleration of the heart rate with one mental difficulty or another.

In this light, it is instructive to examine the central categories of measurement used by the quantified-self culture. Over the past few years, the most popular unit has been the "step," the counting of which no longer even requires a special device (such as a Fitbit wristband). Among the standard features of the most popular smartphones, this function is already preinstalled, as in the "Health" app that has come with every iPhone since the 5s model and cannot be deleted. Whether they are working out or not, the owners of today's smartphones count their steps on a daily basis without controlling these values or even paying much attention to them. Outside of the military context, however, where did this need first arise? Under what conditions did it become necessary in the human sciences to calculate the unit of the "step" with technical precision? In Hans Gross's *Criminal Investigation: A Practical Handbook*, which since its original German publication in 1893 has served as the foundational textbook in the field of criminology, there is a lengthy passage in which Gross explains that the future police investigator "will indeed be unable to 'go for a walk,' in the sense of strolling with mind at rest, enjoying peacefully the beauties of nature." Instead, he goes on, "In all the walks he makes, either for pleasure or duty, an ordnance or survey map should be in his hand."[35] By way of an example, Gross then illustrates why it is important for investigators to pay close and constant attention to routes and distances: "A witness estimates an important distance at, let us say, 200 yards: let him be brought out of doors and say how far might be 100, 200, 300, 400 yards; if now these distances be measured, one can easily judge if and with what degree of accuracy the witness can judge distances."[36] Gross recommends that future criminologists should turn the calculation of distances into a professional priority:

> As this judging of distances is often necessary, it becomes important to measure before-hand from a convenient window certain visible fixed points and to note the distances for future examinations. For years the author had many occasions for doing so from his office-room window and knew for instance: to the left corner of the house – 65 yards; to the poplar tree – 120; to the church spire – 210; to the small house – 400; to the railway – 950. By these distances he has often tested witnesses. If the witness proves fairly accurate in his estimates, his evidence may be considered important for the case under investigation.[37]

Around the beginning of the twentieth century, the police investigator was a human step counter – a Fitbit wristband made of flesh and blood – but this tool was not used to benefit his own well-being but rather to improve the productivity of the justice system. Things would be much easier, according to Gross, if all of this counting did not have to be done by the human investigator himself but could rather be accomplished by technical means. And, in fact, he goes on to discuss just such an apparatus in his *Handbook*. In a section devoted to the "equipment of the investigating officer," he lists what the officer's "travelling office box or bag" ought to contain. One of the items on this list is a so-called pedometer, which he describes as follows: "A *pedometer*, though not perhaps indispensable, is most useful; it is the shape and size of a watch. If one wishes to measure a long distance, one sets the needles on all the dials (units, tens, &c.) at zero, puts the instrument in the pocket and walks off."[38] Gross ends this discussion by addressing the question of where the investigator ought to keep this small apparatus on his body. Although it might seem obvious to wear it around one's wrist, Gross adds the following remark: "For greater certainty one may put the instrument in one's boot, when every step will certainly be registered. Thus better results are obtained than by merely counting paces, while the great advantage accrues that he who carries it can look about him and devote his attention to other matters, which is quite impossible while continually counting."[39] Like precursors to today's users of "Nike+," who slide their GPS-supported step counters into the designated pocket on their running shoe, the police officers envisioned by Gross are supposed to patrol their districts with this new apparatus stuck in their boot. At the beginning of the twentieth century, the "step" thus became an object of exact calculation, and the aim of these calculations was to help police investigators to take control of exceptional situations in which mere places have become crime scenes and every stray detail might provide a crucial piece of evidence.

The automatic step counter kept in Hans Gross's "travelling office box" around the year 1900 (on display at the Museum of Criminology in Graz).

Around this same time, there happened to be another area of science that dealt with exceptional circumstances and likewise placed the "step" at the center of its attention. Unlike criminal investigations, however, in this field the step was not used as an instrument for convicting deviant subjects but was rather treated as an expression of deviance itself. Among the possible manifestations of a certain group of psychopathological symptoms, which Richard Krafft-Ebing referred to as "obsessional ideas" in 1867 and which would be systematically studied a decade later by Carl Westphal, the psychiatrists of the late nineteenth and early twentieth centuries repeatedly described a disorder known variously as "counting compulsion," "obsessive counting," or "arithmomania."[40] If, as in Westphal's classic definition, obsessional ideas are those that "rise to the foreground of consciousness against the will of the affected person, cannot be driven away, and impede and frustrate one's normal train of thought,"[41] then the overwhelming and uncontrollable urge to count things ranks among their most tormenting realizations. Documented cases of arithmomania – in Westphal's work, this phenomenon is still clearly distinguished from the "genuine manias" upon which diagnoses of schizophrenia were based in the early twentieth century[42] – include the compulsive counting of banknotes, spoken words, and people passing by on the street. One of its most common manifestations, however, was the obsessive counting of steps.

In his 1892 dissertation *Über Zwangsvorstellungen* ["On Obsessional Ideas"], for instance, Georg Joachim related the medical history of a 31-year-old woman from Berlin who, after separating from her husband, "found herself in the most miserable situation": "Since that time, she has been compelled, wherever she might be, to divide up every object she sees and to count the number of its constituent parts.... Whenever the patient is out on the sidewalk, she avoids cracks and has to count every cobblestone she steps on. If she fails to satisfy these compulsions, then she is overcome by feelings of great anxiety and discomfort."[43] Around 30 years later, Walter Jahrreiß recorded a number of similar cases, now under the diagnosis of schizophrenia. About the 19-year-old patient "Karl W," he observed: "When walking, he had to compulsively count his steps up to six and then restart at one."[44] About the 57-year-old "Michel S": "Years later, he began to count things, and he did not know the cause of this. At first he counted his steps. In all of this, the number four played a large role. He always calculated whether his steps were divisible by four. If they were not, he grew anxious.... Later, he had to count his steps in such a way that their total number, when added to the number of the day on the calendar, had to yield an odd number."[45] In his notes on an interview with another patient, Jahrreiß wrote: "He stood up from his chair, took a few steps to the left, then said: 'O God, that was all wrong, I should have walked in the other direction.' Then he went to the door and stood before it, hesitated a little, and finally took a big step through the doorway. Then he counted the number of stairs on his way down to the clinic. He considered it very lucky that there happened to be thirteen of them."[46]

Around the year 1900, obsessive step-counting also features in literary depictions of insanity. Alfred Döblin, who was trained as a psychiatrist, began his most famous short story – "The Murder of a Buttercup" (1905) – with the following words: "The gentleman in black had been counting his steps at first, one, two, three, up to a hundred and back again, as he made his way along the wide road edged with firs up to St. Ottilien, swaying so far to right or left with each movement of his hips that he sometimes staggered; then he forgot it."[47] Döblin's portrayal of the businessman Michael Fischer, who frantically hacks off the head of a flower while taking a walk through the woods and is haunted by this act throughout the rest of the story, has been interpreted by literary scholars as "an exact description of obsessional neurosis."[48] The mounting agitation and delusions of the protagonist, however, are anticipated by the arithmomania depicted in the story's opening sentence, an obsession that recurs soon after Fischer is through with his "attack" on the buttercup: "After a short time, he began again to count his steps, one, two, three."[49]

Ever since obsessive ideas and behavior were first noticed, psychiatrists have been trying to explain this peculiar need for "excessive precision" (this is how, at the end of the 1860s, one of the earliest diagnosed patients in Germany described his own condition).[50] "It does not follow from my observations," wrote Carl Westphal in 1877, "that sexual excess of any sort (masturbation, etc.) plays an especially common role in the etiology of this disorder."[51] This opinion, however, would soon be contested by the nascent psychoanalytic interest in obsessive disorders at the end of the nineteenth century. Freud devoted two of his early essays to what he called the "burdensome ceremonial" of counting and other obsessive behaviors. In "The Neuro-Psychoses of Defence," which was published in 1894, he interpreted such disorders as failed attempts to repress early erotic stimulations: "In hysteria, the incompatible idea is rendered innocuous by its sum of excitation being transformed into something somatic" – something such as obsessive impulses.[52] Two years later, in "Further Remarks on the Neuro-Psychoses of Defence," Freud expressed this notion in clearer terms: "The nature of obsessional neurosis can be expressed in a simple formula. Obsessional ideas are invariably transformed self-reproaches which have re-emerged from repression and which always relate to some sexual act that was performed with pleasure in childhood."[53]

However the meticulous counting of one's own steps happened to be understood around the year 1900 – whether as an unsuccessful process of repression or in the sense proposed by the French psychiatrist Alexandre Cullerre, who believed that epileptic and depressed patients would at first make use of arithmomania "as a way to free themselves from their bleak thoughts, and then this originally arbitrary act would gradually develop into an irresistible impulse to make pointless calculations"[54] – this activity, at least when it was not employed to reconstruct the events of a crime, was always attributed to compunctions that were thought to be imposed upon those engaged in it. There is a reason, after all, why the medical community categorized this activity as a *compulsive* disorder, as it still does. The impulse to count things in a constant manner is one that overpowers the subject in question; it threatens to take away the subject's sovereignty over his or her perception and mental faculties. What is more, the results of the subject's own addictive counting cannot be trusted, as Leopold Löwenfeld pointed out in 1904. In a case study of a patient who, among other things, "counted his pulse and how often he swallowed saliva," Leopold observed: "These tallies were … purely imaginary; the patient's results never agreed with his actual heart rate."[55] Psychiatrists around the turn of the twentieth century, in other words, did not even trust the data that their arithmomanic patients collected in their own minds.

The rampant and collective step-counting in today's digital culture – the current obsession with wearing Fitbit devices and monitoring health apps on smartphones – is no longer an inner compulsion but rather a voluntary decision. A pathological disposition has transformed into a desire for fitness; "self-reproaches which have re-emerged from repression," in the sexual sense, have transformed into a program of self-empowerment. In the obsessive "observation of numbers" characteristic of neurotics, Freud suspected that certain "penitential measures" were at work.[56] Yet for what sins are the millions of health-conscious people today, glued as they are to their wearables, supposed to be performing penance?

Measuring, classifying, discriminating

In the late nineteenth and early twentieth centuries, the scientific focus of measuring techniques on identifying deviance ultimately led to a widespread enthusiasm for discrediting and marginalizing entire portions of the human population by means of bodily measurements. Around 35 years ago, the historian of science Stephen Jay Gould wrote a highly acclaimed book, *The Mismeasure of Man*, about these effective and influential efforts. Gould's study is a piercing critique of the "biological determinism" espoused by Broca, Lombroso, and the twentieth-century inventors of intelligence tests: "I would rather label the whole enterprise of setting a biological value upon groups for what it is: irrelevant, intellectually unsound, and highly injurious."[57] His analyses are concerned above all with two fundamental fallacies that have influenced the measurement of intelligence in fields such as craniometry and quantitative psychology: on the one hand, the practice of *reification* (the scientific tendency "to convert an abstract concept ... into a hard entity"); on the other hand, the practice of *ranking* ("our propensity for ordering complex variation as a gradually ascending scale").[58] This dual reduction of heterogeneous phenomena (such as intelligence) to a "unitary 'thing,'"[59] which can then be placed within a specific ranking, is what led to "the mismeasure of man" and thus inspired the title of Gould's book. These methodological deficiencies are consequential, he believes, because craniometry or Goddard's and Terman's intelligence tests did not use numbers to advance objective knowledge but rather to confirm social prejudices and "illustrate a priori conclusions."[60] Rankings such as "white – black – ape" or "upright citizen – criminal – ape" had already been established features of Broca's and Lombroso's social-Darwinian worldview long before their many measurements provided ostensible evidence to confirm their ideologically motivated hypotheses.

Even if Gould's approach raises certain methodological questions of its own – he, too, is interested in gathering evidence to prove a-priori hypotheses, and in many places he simply trumps criticized historical results with more accurate measurements of his own – his book is nevertheless an important point of reference for the issues under discussion. First and foremost, it makes it easy to see the differences between the quantitative sciences in the decades around 1900 and the self-tracking techniques in digital culture. Like the scientists described by Gould, today's proponents of the quantified self consider themselves "servants of their numbers,"[61] but their use of such data has nothing at all to do with explaining social strata or marginalizing certain groups. This difference is especially clear in the concept of "disposition," the understanding of which has shifted. For craniometrists and the American popularizers of intelligence tests, the biological (and, as of the 1880s, genetic) endowment of human beings was the decisive factor in their development and social status. The *being* of the criminal or problematic schoolboy was everything, and this was registered in the shape of his skull, the size of his brain, and in his genetic material, while his *becoming*, which was shaped by external and dynamic factors, was utterly ignored. Gould thus refers to the quantitative sciences under consideration with the fitting term "theories of limits": they assert that the quantifiable differences between ethnicities, genders, or populations are not only innate but, above all, immutable.[62] Such a classification, however, which is determined by nature and cannot be overcome by the individual, contradicts all of the basic principles of the quantified-self culture, which is concerned with permanently shifting and optimizing limits in order to satisfy, day by day and step by step, the wishful thinking of leading a more healthy, productive, and fulfilling life.

From cementing the boundaries between groups on the basis of data to expanding the limits of individuals on the basis of data – this broad arc seems to separate the earlier quantitative sciences from the self-trackers of today. A closer look, however, reveals certain similarities in their respective methods and motivations, and the distance between them begins to shrink. In Gould's book, categories such as the "cranial index" or the "intelligence quotient" receive such harsh criticism because they convert a multifaceted phenomenon into a "measurable entity."[63] Is it not possible to understand concepts such as Generali's "Vitality points" or Decadoo's "health score" as reductive categories of the same sort? Complex realities such as "health" or "mood," which vary from one person to the next, seem to be treated here as precisely calculable and universally valid quantities. The two methodological fallacies that Gould identifies in historical efforts to measure intelligence – again, reification and ranking – seem to apply just as well to today's measurements of health and wellness.

At the same time, while the quantified-self project might at first glance seem to focus on the individual, its aims have shifted more and more toward accessing collectives. Unlike in the efforts of Broca, Lombroso, or Goddard, the issue here is not one of deploying biology to legitimate the minority status of women, blacks, criminals, or the poor. Based on digital self-monitoring, these new insurance programs are rather intended to differentiate other types of groups – namely, the healthy from the sick, the fit from the unfit, the cautious from the negligent. This has resulted in new hierarchies or rankings, and although they are not meant to represent any innate classifications, they nevertheless correspond to those of the earlier quantitative sciences in an important respect: their omission of socio-economic factors. A century ago, Lewis Terman, who revised the Stanford–Binet IQ test, expressed his conviction that "class boundaries had been set by innate intelligence."[64] When Gary Wolf introduced his four terms – again, "thin," "rich," "happy," and "smart" – as the leading goals of self-tracking, he likewise evoked an inner human authority: not innate intelligence, as in Terman's case, but rather sheer determination or willpower, which he thus implied is stronger than any social force. According to Terman's argument, people remain poor on account of their lower intelligence; according to Wolf, the poor are those who lack sufficient motivation and self-discipline. Clearly, these are not categorically different positions. The social Darwinism of skull and brain measurers seems to have transformed today into a sort of mentality-based Darwinism, and in this sense it is no coincidence that one of the recent advertisements by Fitbit depicts the "evolution" of its tracking devices by alluding to the famous scientific illustration known as "The March of Progress."

An advertisement on Fitbit's website (2017).

If the aim of the influential corporations in digital culture truly is to create a "new man," then the motif of this advertisement – more than being just a playful allusion – illustrates this ambition with unusual clarity. Such genealogies place the community of self-trackers in a difficult situation. As is well known, this is a community defined by its political and moral sensitivity and by its anti-racist and anti-sexist principles. Yet, in the early twenty-first century, its members are busy perpetuating certain measuring practices that were devised in the late nineteenth century in the name of sexism, racism, and social discrimination.

Introspection and data generation

In his manifesto for the quantified-self movement, as we have seen, Gary Wolf distinguished the act of measuring one's own body from the "prolix, literary humanism" of psychoanalysis, and he contrasted the language-based efforts of psychoanalysts to delve into the deep layers of human consciousness with the practice of making technical recordings "of our most trivial thoughts and actions."[65] By formulating these juxtapositions, Wolf was in fact reviving an old methodological dispute about the most effective ways to study human beings. This dispute, as you might by now expect, was at its hottest around the year 1900. In their case studies, Freud and Breuer demonstrated the power of the "talking cure," which enables analysts to treat hysterical bodily symptoms by prompting patients to recall formative memories and thereby come to terms with neurotic complexes. According to this notion of therapy, the self is an ensemble of biographical impressions, some of which have been processed better than others, and the art of psychoanalysis lies in exhuming the origins of painful and "repressed" impressions from the past.

In the early twentieth century, however, this hermeneutic approach to the inner life of human beings – this somewhat vertical perspective on its secrets and riddles – was opposed in the human sciences by a horizontal approach that was no less influential. Disciplines such as experimental psychology and its derivative schools (including psychotechnics and behaviorism) were not deeply interested in accessing human beings via language or in discovering the biographical origins of disorders; their aim was rather to stimulate and record the superficial expressions of the human body. Instead of plumbing the introspection of their patients, they measured them; instead of producing memories and words, they focused on the production of body currents and data; instead of waiting around for the delayed outbreak of latent complexes, they were concerned with immediate reactions to external stimuli. These currents and reactions were so subtle, however, that they could not be registered by human perception. As Hugo Münsterberg noted in 1914, for instance, "the evidence that even the slightest fluctuations in feeling are reflected in changes to one's blood circulation, in involuntary muscle movements, and in the activity of one's sweat glands" is difficult to detect, and technical instruments are therefore needed to make the bodily expressions of mental activity "perceptible where they might escape the usual attention of the viewer."[66] From the beginning, then, quantitative psychology required the assistance of apparatuses and technical media. Pulse recorders, blood-pressure recorders and pneumographs did the work that psychoanalysts hoped to accomplish with just their ears, a pen, and some paper. To the extent that certain human sciences lost faith in the ability of people to reveal things about themselves by means of memories and language, increased efforts were thus made to use technology in order to assemble some sort of truth from the fragmented signals produced by the human body.

Beside Münsterberg's psychotechnics, one of the sharpest critics of the hermeneutic approach to the inner lives of human beings was behaviorist psychology, which was developed in the United States. Whereas Wilhelm Wundt's experimental school had been busy taking exact measurements of human consciousness since the 1870s, John Watson, the founder of behaviorism, took things a step further by eliminating the category of consciousness altogether. In his essay "Psychology as the Behaviorist Views It," which was published in 1913, he declared: "The time seems to have come when psychology must discard all reference to consciousness; when it need no longer delude itself into thinking that it is making mental states the object of observation."[67] The only thing that experimental psychology ever accomplished, in his view, "was to substitute for the word 'soul' the word 'consciousness.'"[68] Instead of hunting for some mysterious psychological essence of man, Watson preferred the pragmatic approach of simply studying human activity and behavior. Like the experimental psychologists before him, he studied the relation between "stimulus" and "response" – between external impulses and internal transformations of human behavior – but he did so not to illuminate our inner being but rather to identify recurring behavioral patterns. The only concern of behaviorism was to observe and measure effects; regarding the subjective and emotional origins of these effects, it had no interest whatsoever. "Its theoretical goal," as Watson explained about the new science, "is the prediction and control of behavior."[69]

The aspiring methods of behaviorism, which became one of the most influential schools of psychology, can be seen as a direct critique of the representational approach used by language-oriented psychology. In this view, words are dubious emissaries of the inner condition; to behaviorists, the culture of language seemed too convoluted to provide an adequate illustration of the instantaneous relationship between stimuli and reactions. B. F. Skinner, who was long the most preeminent representative of the behaviorist school, repeatedly underscored the incongruity between the inner life of emotions and linguistic expression. As far as he was concerned, feelings should simply be understood as reactions to stimuli, but reports about them should be regarded as the result of particular linguistic contingencies related to the society in question: "We cannot measure sensations and perceptions as such," he wrote, "but we can measure a person's capacity to discriminate among stimuli, and the concept of sensation or perception can then be reduced to the operation of discrimination."[70]

In this light, the connections between today's quantified-self methods and the perspectives of psychotechnics and behaviorism are especially clear. Today's self-trackers likewise consider language to be an unreliable medium for understanding human beings. Fitness wristbands, smart watches, and apps used to quantify one's mood are intended to provide information about their users by means of data produced by their own bodies. Ulrich Raulff once described the establishment of quantitative psychology as an act of "turning away from questions of being toward questions of cause and effect."[71] This same constellation motivates the culture of self-tracking, with its ubiquitous recordings, yet there is one important difference that is central to the conception of human beings in the culture of digital self-recording. In their work, behaviorists such as Watson and Skinner repeatedly stress that the shift of their psychological interest from "consciousness" to "behavior" involves a radical critique of the autonomous subject. In Skinner's understanding of psychology, for instance, there is no room for the idea of independent agency. A person should rather be understood as a sort of intersection: "[H]e is a locus, a place at which many genetic and environmental conditions come together in a joint effect."[72] He asserts, moreover: "There is no place in the scientific position for a self as a true originator or initiator of action."[73] There is thus a glaring paradox in the culture of self-tracking: although it has adopted the epistemological principles of psychotechnics and behaviorism, thus regarding human beings as producers of superficial data whose inner lives defy scrutiny, it somehow draws entirely different conclusions from these practices about the status of the subject. By recording and managing his or her own blood pressure, heart rate, and daily movement, the "quantified self" is supposed to become the very "originator or initiator of action" that Skinner had outright dismissed. Here we encounter the same discontinuity as that which characterized the transformation of the electronic ankle bracelet into the GPS-equipped smartphone: The technical ensemble is more or less the same, and the basic function of recording remains intact, but, in both cases, a former instrument of control was transformed into a tool of self-empowerment. This historical similarity between the methods for determining someone's location and those for measuring bodies is all the more apparent in the fact that, as mentioned above, it was one of B. F. Skinner's students, Ralph Schwitzgebel, who in the late 1960s had developed the first prototype of the electronic ankle bracelet. His aim in doing so, moreover, was to implement a form of "behavioral control," which was of course the principle goal of behaviorism as stated by John Watson. The apparatuses, technologies, and even the methodological counterparts of self-tracking (such as psychoanalysis) are thus all part of the same scientific lineage. It is not for nothing that the Generali insurance company has advertised its "Vitality" program with the following words: "Vitality is a unique behavioral-based shared value insurance model,"[74] though with the opposite promise of promoting the *autonomy* of its customers by means of behavioristic control mechanisms.

Tied up with this paradox is the issue of the methodological complications posed by measuring oneself. In the scientific disciplines whose premises are borrowed by the quantified-self culture, it is generally regarded as a dubious practice to unite the measuring authority and the object of measurement into a single entity. Hugo Münsterberg repeatedly stressed the need to have professional guidance in all psychotechnical experiments; an "untrained average person," he wrote, would be incapable of executing the measurements.[75] John Watson, too, made a similarly categorical remark in his introductory lecture on behaviorism: "You will soon find that instead of self-observation being the easiest and most natural way of studying psychology, it is an impossible one; you can observe in yourselves only the most elementary forms of response. You will find, on the other hand, that when you begin to study what your neighbor is doing, you will rapidly become proficient in giving a reason for his behavior."[76] B. F. Skinner was of the same opinion: "In self-knowledge, the knowing self is different from the known. In self-management, the controlling self is different from the controlled."[77]

Today's self-tracking movement is not at all bothered by such basic methodological debates. For the companies who make the products and the customers who use them, it is beyond any doubt that the measurement methods of smartphones and their accompanying apps provide reliable and useful data. This collective trust, however, is frequently and clearly refuted by the very medical disciplines whose research depends on measuring the phenomena in question. So far, the sharpest critique of the devices and apps used by the quantified-self movement has come from professional sleep researchers. As mentioned above, one of the functions of current fitness wristbands like Fitbit and special apps such as Sleep Bot, Wake Mate, Sleep Advisor, or Sleep as Android is to provide accurate measurements and recordings of the quantity and quality of one's sleep. According to the descriptions of these products, such measurements require no effort whatsoever; it is enough to keep a smartphone near your body or wear a fitness band overnight, and, simply on the basis of your movements, these devices supposedly produce an informative protocol of the restful or restless stages of your slumber. "Use a Fitbit tracker to record your sleep at night," the company's website recommends: "Then, use the sleep tools in the app to set a weekly sleep goal, create bedtime reminders and wake targets, and review your sleep trends over time."[78]

The deficiencies of these recording techniques have been described more and more in recent years. All that the sensors in wristbands or apps are able to register are the body's movements throughout the night, which are then tabulated and graphed out to illustrate the soundness of someone's sleep. Measurements of this sort are utterly crude in comparison with the work of medical sleep researchers, who have been monitoring brain waves and REM cycles since the middle of the twentieth century. Published in 1968 by the American Department of Health, the first manual devoted to standardizing the terminology employed in the field of sleep research states that the scientific quality of any sleep assessment can only be guaranteed so long as the activity of each patient is recorded by at least one electroencephalogram, one electromyogram of the chin, and two electrooculograms of the eyes.[79] Compared to the data produced by such techniques, of course, the meager informative value of the data created by self-tracking devices cannot be denied. In light of the obvious nature of this discrepancy, however, perhaps it is more interesting to ask why these devices and apps, whose inaccuracy is no secret to their users, have enjoyed such great success. There seems to exist a general yearning to record things in digital culture, a tendency toward self-Taylorization that outweighs even our awareness of the unreliability of the measurements themselves. This peculiar longing, moreover, has suppressed other perspectives about new technologies, which were once influential during the early stages of the digital age – for instance, the fear concerning the potential health risks posed by the devices, not least that of their "radiation," which was a big issue in the discussions about so-called "electrosmog" that were widespread around the turn of the twenty-first century. The website of the sleep-tracking app Sleep as Android makes the following suggestion about where the phone should be positioned overnight: "The phone needs to keep contact with the mattress in order to capture your movements. We recommend putting it on the mattress near your body. Good positions include: under the pillow."[80] In other words: keep the phone next to your head! Just 15 years ago, such remarks would have mobilized a slew of cultural critics and citizen action groups. By now, however, the desire for self-measurement has canceled out any fears we might have about the unpredictable effects of technologically induced radiation.

Lifting the veil

In order to explain why the quantified-self movement, with all of its emphasis on individual agency, happens to rely on sciences that have historically treated the measured subject as an utterly passive entity, it will be helpful to revisit once more Gary Wolf's essay from 2010. In this text, he cites someone who has been meticulously tracking his own alcohol consumption with an electronic diary. By entrusting this information to a computer instead of to another person, he allegedly bypassed the threat of social shame and was thus less likely to underestimate his drinking. Wolf's comment about this man's realization is as follows: "After all, it is silly to posture in front of a machine."[81] This statement underscores the essentially unproblematic relation that self-trackers have to the truth. If the person doing the measuring is identical to the person being measured, there is supposedly no reason to doubt the willingness of the test subject to produce reliable data. For self-trackers, one's inner life and one's external bodily signals exist in perfect harmony. The person leading the investigation and the object of the investigation itself are accomplices.

This complicity, however, represents a crucial difference between today's passion for self-recording and its background in the history of science. In the fields of anthropometry, psychotechnics, and behavioral electronics, the relationship between the person taking measurements and the person being measured was one of rivalry. The instruments and methods developed around the year 1900 were meant to uncover hidden knowledge. "Under certain conditions," wrote Hugo Münsterberg, "both doctors and legal practitioners have an interest in bringing to light thoughts and moods that are being kept secret."[82] Behind this veil, he thought, lies the true nature of psychiatric disorders and the guiltiness or true identity of a criminal suspect – things that, though not openly expressed by the people under investigation, could be revealed by the length of their bones or the charts produced by their bodily currents. These quantitative sciences were based on the presumption that patients or suspects were inclined to refute themselves: what they left unspoken, that is, could supposedly be demonstrated by their heart rates or by radius of their skulls. In the rhetoric of these sciences, bodily manifestations were congruent with the content of the mind.

What was it at the end of the nineteenth century that gave rise to so many instruments designed to establish the truth? Looking into the matter, one finds that these developments were largely motivated by the unreliability of witness statements. It was this phenomenon, in fact, that necessitated the alliance between applied psychology and the criminal justice system. With its countless digressions about criminal psychology and the art of detecting clues, Hans Gross's *Criminal Investigation: A Practical Handbook* is primarily an effect brought about by this "crisis of the witness" around 1900. Writing around the same time, Hugo Münsterberg remarked: "It is perhaps no exaggeration to say that there is even a new special science that deals exclusively with the reliability of memory."[83] The main contribution of psychotechnics was its invention of methods and apparatuses for overcoming this lack of reliability – "prosthetic means of establishing the truth," which, as Münsterberg believed, were more trustworthy than the fragmentary statements of witnesses or the often violently coerced confessions of suspects.[84] "Everyday life," he wrote, "provides all sorts of opportunities to observe how feelings, often unintentionally or even against the intentions of individuals, are expressed in involuntary behavior and in the perceptible functions of the circulatory system and sweat glands. When we see how a person blushes or turns pale upon hearing a particular name – how tears well in his eyes, his speech begins to stutter, and his hands begin to quiver – we can regard these things as symptoms of inner agitation."[85] The aim here was thus to formulate a reliable semiotics of guilt. As in Broca's or Lombroso's work a half-century before, this was based on a clear representational relationship between bodily signals and inner conditions. Unlike Broca and Lombroso, however, Münsterberg was not interested in incontrovertible biological conditions, which he rejected, but rather in the fleeting emotional states of people under interrogation.

Convinced that changes in a person's complexion, heart rate, or pace of breathing are precise reflections of his or her inner life, Münsterberg designed a so-called polygraph, the prototype of today's lie detectors. Withheld truth and concealed guilt – inner complexes that Freud, working at the same time, was attempting to detect and resolve by listening to his patients' words – could now be revealed by means of an apparatus. In this case, the code of translation was clear: regular frequencies and steady lines on the chart signified probity and innocence, while any abrupt spikes were signs of suspicion that indicated inner discord. Admittedly, Hugo Münsterberg was cautious enough to take into account the risk of misinterpretation, stating that "symptoms of mere agitation, which the legal process can bring about in the innocent as well, can be misinterpreted as signs of guilt."[86] Yet, despite these reservations, he considered the polygraph to be an apparatus that was far more reliable than any previous methods for extracting the truth, such as the use of torture "to wrest the facts of the case from the soul of the accused."[87]

Up to his death in 1916, Münsterberg was regularly called upon to testify in courts of law as an expert in psychology. During the years around the First World War, his studies with the polygraph machine were refined by other scholars, and, beginning in the 1930s, the apparatus came to be used widely by the American justice system. The reputation of the "lie detector" at this time was that of a merciless device that could cut through any attempted resistance to reveal even the most deeply hidden secrets; accordingly, suspects and doubtful witnesses were not leaping at the chance to be subjected to this bodily interrogation. (Even years later, at the beginning of the Watergate scandal, Richard Nixon was quoted as saying, "I don't know anything about polygraphs, and I don't know how accurate they are, but I know they'll scare the hell out of people.")[88] Delinquents had to be hooked up by force to the truth-telling machine; in this context, the measurements can only be seen as the result of an act of coercion undertaken against the will of the subject.

This ensemble of bodies could not have differed more from the other established ritual at the time for extracting the truth – namely, the psychoanalytic session. In his essay on the achievements of Hugo Münsterberg, Ulrich Raulff provides an excellent juxtaposition of these two emblematic scenes from the early-twentieth-century human sciences. In the office of the psychoanalyst, the patient lies down on a sofa and the analyst sits behind him or her and takes notes – the postures are comfortable, the cushions are soft, and there is no eye contact or physical contact between the people involved. And then there is the scene with the polygraph, which takes place in a sparse and brightly lit room. The examiner sits across from the subject, who is perhaps being restrained by police officers, and in between them there is a device that is attached to the subject with multiple wires. "If you are unable or unwilling to tell the truth," writes Raulff, "perhaps you will simply sweat it out? This is not to say that language no longer plays any role here. The role has merely changed from engaging in a protracted wrestling match with meaning to performing a verbal vivisection. Like little lancets or thorns, key words are thrust against a body that has to be pierced in order for the secret truth to emerge."[89] From today's perspective, it is interesting that Raulff, in any essay written more than 30 years ago, did not hesitate to depict this comparison as an opposition between willingness and coercion, conversation and interrogation. Psychoanalysis takes place as an agreement between the doctor and the patient; polygraph measurements are a struggle in which the lying delinquent has to bend to the machine's powers of veracity. In the age of the quantified self, these two independent methods have in some sense come together. Just as the patients of an analyst typically come to his or her practice willingly, today's self-trackers wear their costly Fitbit wristbands of their own volition. As Gary Wolf has insinuated, the subject in this case is still regarded as someone lacking something, but it is no longer a lack of honesty or an unwillingness to confess that has created the need for such measuring devices. Rather, it is the lack of attention being paid to one's own fitness and one's own well-being.

Witnesses for the prosecution

Despite all the invocations of the autonomous subject, the way that digital self-recording functions is always easiest to see when the individually generated data enter a broader context of knowledge encompassing more than the individual. The current bonus programs offered by insurance companies have made this clear. Methods of self-tracking may indeed help the individual to improve his or her health and productivity, but at the same time these collected data emanate outward – not because of misuse and not because of carelessness, but rather because the practice of the quantified self has been situated, from its beginning, within large-scale networks. In the insurance industry, such data can be used to make precise assertions about a given user's state of health; the measurements are thus taken to represent a sort of truth about his or her "normality," thereby perpetuating a scientific presumption whose roots extend back to the nineteenth century. Recently, however, another application of fitness bands has emerged that makes these genealogies even clearer by transferring the "truth" in its juridical sense, which is the sense that Bertillon and Münsterberg had in mind, into the era of the quantified self. Fitbit devices, in other words, are now being admitted as evidence in courts of law.

At the end of 2014, a personal injury claim was made in Ottawa by a fitness trainer who, on account of an accident suffered four years earlier, could no longer continue in her line of work. Among other evidence submitted to the court was the plaintiff's Fitbit device, which was intended to demonstrate, according to her lawyers, "that her activity levels are still lower than the baseline of her age and profession to show that she deserves compensation."[90] The lawyers also presented comparative information gathered by a company that evaluates self-tracking data for the insurance industry, and thus they were able to use statistics to demonstrate the physical impairment of their client. This Canadian case, which was ultimately decided in favor of the claimant, was apparently the first legal process worldwide in which data from a fitness wristband were used as evidence. On the one hand, the ruling seems to attest to the new sovereignty of self-trackers, given that the Fitbit sensors supported the legitimacy of the claim more dependably than any statement from a medical expert ever could have.[91] On the other hand, the case represents an important threshold in digital culture to the extent that it illustrates that the personal data collected by a self-tracking instrument can be transformed at any time from its playful and innocent function of counting calories into a legally admissible piece of evidence in a court case. Kate Crawford, a journalist who followed the proceedings, was quick to point out the important implications of this change. Although in Ottawa, she wrote, the Fitbit device may have been used to support the plaintiff's injury claim, "wearables data could just as easily be used by insurers to deny disability claims, or by prosecutors seeking a rich source of self-incriminating evidence.... Will it change people's relationship to their wearable device when they know that it can be an informant?"[92] The colorful Fitbit wristband has become an instrument that preventatively counts its wearer's every step in order to make it easier, one day, to apprehend him in the event of one violation or another.

In fact, the first case of this sort took place in April 2015. A woman from Pennsylvania claimed to have been pulled out of her bed and sexually assaulted by a stranger. Over the course of the investigation, however, the police became aware that she had been wearing her Fitbit device during the night in question, and she permitted them to analyze the data. The latter made it unmistakably clear that she had been awake and active during the supposed time of the crime. The case was dismissed, and the claimant was ordered to pay a fine for having issued a false statement. "Never lie while wearing a Fitbit," as one American reporter commented on the case.[93] Today's self-tracking devices are polygraphs that are more comprehensive and exhaustive in scope than anything Hugo Münsterberg could have imagined. And whereas the measured delinquents of the twentieth century had to be hooked up to polygraphs by force, the millions of customers using Fitbit, Jawbone, Nike+, and other truth-telling wearables do so willingly. As one writer remarked about the plaintiff in the Pennsylvania case: "[T]he device became a witness against her."[94] Even if the playful applications of today's self-tracking devices make it easy to forget their historical background, their original intention still occasionally rises to the surface.

4

The Forgotten Fear of Registration

The drama of the census

One of the largest protest movements in the history of West Germany took shape in early 1987. Coordinated by the Green Party, up to 1,500 "initiative groups" were formed throughout the country, and hundreds of thousands of participants gathered at demonstrations. The cause of this collective protest was the national census that was scheduled to begin on May 25 that year. "Few efforts on the part of the Bonn government have incited so much resistance and aggression," wrote the *Spiegel* magazine about the plan to take stock of approximately 25 million households by means of some 600,000 official census takers.[1] The acts of resistance were varied and inventive. One night before a soccer match, an unidentified group of people broke into the stadium in Dortmund and painted the words "Boycott the census" on the playing field. Because there was not enough time to remove this message before the opening whistle, officials changed it to "Don't boycott the census" in a desperate effort to promote the upcoming event. In West Berlin, activists gathered at the border of the divided city and, indifferent to the threats of fines, glued all of their survey forms to the Berlin Wall. The initiative groups distributed countless pamphlets and brochures listing strategies for sabotaging the mechanical readability of the census forms (cutting their edges, spilling coffee on them, etc.).

All of this protest energy was released because, in the eyes of many, the planned survey was at odds with the fundamental rights of the democratic state. In their preface to a book titled *Was Sie gegen Mikrozensus und Volkszählung tun können* ["What You Can Do Against the Micro-Census and the National Census"], which sold more than 250,000 copies by April of 1987, the editors mention, for instance, "a tightly woven surveillance network that will soon be draped over all citizens." "The goal," they continue, "is the total surveillance of everyone and the control of future behavior. A fundamental precondition for this is the comprehensive registration of all the data concerning the population."[2] Later on, they state in a similar vein: "The datafication of the entire population of the Federal Republic of Germany will form the material basis for total social control. And control is the first step toward manipulation."[3] All of the key words of the critique against the census can be found in this work and are repeated page after page: "registration," "control," "surveillance," "manipulation." It was the concern of the census's opponents that it would ultimately enable the police and the government administration to treat individuals as passive objects. "Almost without noticing, we are all being turned into puppets,"[4] the editors point out with a frequently used metaphor: "We must defend ourselves against government measures to degrade us into externally controlled puppets."[5]

The protests in 1987 were a continuation of an intense conflict that had begun four years earlier. According to the original plan, the census, which was to be the first since 1970, was scheduled to commence on April 27, 1983. Yet the unanimously ratified "Census Act," which the West German parliament passed in early 1982, encountered unexpected popular resistance just a few months before the process was set to begin. The census, as the President of the Federal Statistical Office commented at the time, "has become an object of public debate to a greater extent than anyone involved had anticipated."[6] By March 1983, the Federal Constitutional Court had received more than 1,200 appeals claiming that the forthcoming census represented a violation of basic rights (including the right "to the free development of one's personality" and the right to "freedom of expression"). One of the latter, which had been submitted by two lawyers and a law student from Hamburg, was heard in court, and on April 13, just two weeks before the process was set to commence, the judges in Karlsruhe suspended the census on account of its unconstitutionality.

In their final ruling, which was issued in December 1983, the judges mandated that any future census activity would have to conform to the "supplementary legal regulations for the execution and organization of data acquisition." Thus the "General Right to Personality" (*Allgemeines Persönlichkeitsrecht*) stipulates that "no connection can be made between collected data and any individualizable person or group of persons." Unlike with the census of 1970, however, it was now possible to establish such connections by means of the new "technical preconditions of data acquisition and data processing."[7] Interconnected at the state and federal levels, electronic registries of the population would have made it possible to identify the personal information provided by any given citizen, and it was precisely this permeability, which the government expressly hoped to build into the new census, that the judges deemed illegal. In the ruling from December 1983, this skepticism about the census's constitutionality even led to the formulation of a new law, namely the aforementioned "right to informational self-determination," which was intended to guarantee the protection of human dignity in the age of electronic data processing. In Germany, this basic right ultimately gave rise to the public discourse about "data protection" and provided guidelines for reformulated census procedures.

The provisions of the Federal Constitutional Court were incorporated into the census documents from 1987, which consisted of a "personal form," a "residential form" and a "household form." Compared with the census planned in 1983, fundamental changes were made to the way in which data would be collected and processed. The names and address of the members of a household, for instance, were no longer to be recorded on the back of the "residential form," as had been the plan four years earlier, but rather on the new "household form," which, after being submitted, would be separated from the other forms by officials. Its sole purpose, according to the text on the form itself, was "to ensure the comprehensiveness of the census; it will not be stored in electronic databases together with the personal form or the residential form." In addition, citizens were now permitted to submit the forms to the authorities on their own instead of having to fill them out in the presence of a census taker, as had been expected in 1983. Finally, stricter guidelines were put in place regarding the electronic processing of the data. On the cover page of the census forms, households were now informed that, in every district, "only the specially designated data collection office" will have access to the surveys: "No other administrative authority and no other municipal or regional agency will be able to view the personal information. It will not be possible to identify any individual on the basis of the information stored at the regional office."[8] The presentation of the new forms was clearly affected by the long debates over "informational self-determination." By 1987, the government had decided to address the people in a tone of appeasement.

Yet what, exactly, did the state want to know that aroused so much collective outrage in the 1980s? For large portions of the population, the total of 33 questions on the surveys – 18 on the "personal form," 11 on the "residential form," with 4 supplementary questions for the owners or managers of buildings – represented an immense threat. During the weeks before May 25, 1987, the struggle against this threat led to the bombing of government offices in which the printed forms were being stored (in Leverkusen and Freiburg, among other places). The census bureaus in the state of Hessia, according to one official involved, thus had to be fortified "like Fort Knox."[9] Looking back at these forms today, now over 30 years after the protests, one might struggle to understand what all of the fuss was about. From today's perspective, that is, the questions on the "personal form" and the "residential form" hardly seem prying at all. In addition to the sort of information contained on any piece of ID, all the state wanted to know were a few things about one's education, profession, commute to work, apartment size and monthly rent. The most intimate information requested on the "personal form" was presumably the response to Question 14: "How much time do you typically need to travel to work or school/college?"

Just a decade after the census, the first social networks began to request personal information of an entirely different order. As mentioned in my first chapter, the patent application for SixDegrees specifies that new members are encouraged to create a profile listing their "e-mail address(es), last name, first name, aliases, occupation, geography, hobbies, skills or

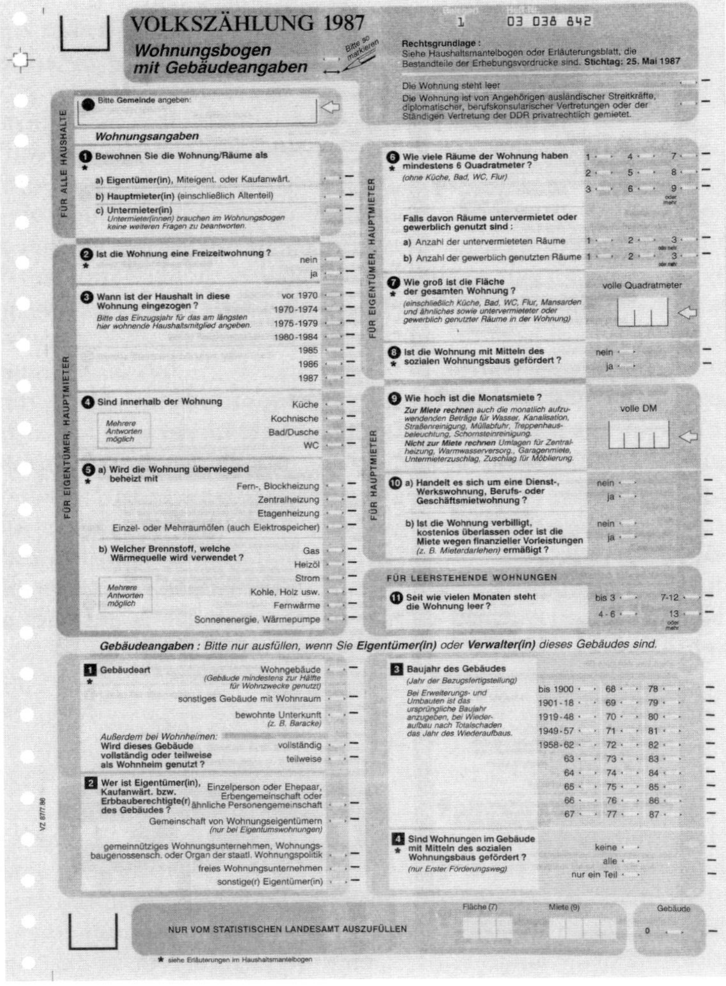

VOLKSZÄHLUNG 1987
Wohnungsbogen mit Gebäudeangaben
Bitte so markieren
1 03 038 842
Rechtsgrundlage:
Siehe Haushaltsmantelbogen oder Erläuterungsblatt, die Bestandteile der Erhebungsvordrucke sind. Stichtag: 25. Mai 1987
Die Wohnung steht leer
Die Wohnung ist von Angehörigen ausländischer Streitkräfte, diplomatischer, berufskonsularischer Vertretungen oder der Ständigen Vertretung der DDR privatrechtlich gemietet.

FÜR ALLE HAUSHALTE
Bitte Gemeinde angeben:
Wohnungsangaben
1 Bewohnen Sie die Wohnung/Räume als *
a) Eigentümer(in), Miteigent. oder Kaufanwärt.
b) Hauptmieter(in) (einschließlich Altenteil)
c) Untermieter(in)
Untermieter(innen) brauchen im Wohnungsbogen keine weiteren Fragen zu beantworten.

FÜR EIGENTÜMER, HAUPTMIETER
2 Ist die Wohnung eine Freizeitwohnung? * nein / ja
3 Wann ist der Haushalt in diese Wohnung eingezogen?
Bitte das Einzugsjahr für das am längsten hier wohnende Haushaltsmitglied angeben.
vor 1970 / 1970-1974 / 1975-1979 / 1980-1984 / 1985 / 1986 / 1987
4 Sind innerhalb der Wohnung
Mehrere Antworten möglich
Küche / Kochnische / Bad/Dusche / WC
5 a) Wird die Wohnung überwiegend beheizt mit *
Fern-, Blockheizung / Zentralheizung / Etagenheizung / Einzel- oder Mehrraumöfen (auch Elektrospeicher)
b) Welcher Brennstoff, welche Wärmequelle wird verwendet?
Mehrere Antworten möglich
Gas / Heizöl / Strom / Kohle, Holz usw. / Fernwärme / Sonnenenergie, Wärmepumpe

FÜR EIGENTÜMER, HAUPTMIETER
6 Wie viele Räume der Wohnung haben mindestens 6 Quadratmeter? *
(ohne Küche, Bad, WC, Flur)
1 / 2 / 3 / 4 / 5 / 6 / 7 / 8 / 9 oder mehr
Falls davon Räume untervermietet oder gewerblich genutzt sind:
a) Anzahl der untervermieteten Räume 1 / 2 / 3 oder mehr
b) Anzahl der gewerblich genutzten Räume 1 / 2 / 3 oder mehr
7 Wie groß ist die Fläche der gesamten Wohnung? *
(einschließlich Küche, Bad, WC, Flur, Mansarden und ähnliches sowie untervermieteter oder gewerblich genutzter Räume in der Wohnung)
volle Quadratmeter
8 Ist die Wohnung mit Mitteln des sozialen Wohnungsbaus gefördert? * nein / ja

FÜR HAUPTMIETER
9 Wie hoch ist die Monatsmiete?
Zur Miete rechnen auch die monatlich aufzuwendenden Beträge für Wasser, Kanalisation, Straßenreinigung, Müllabfuhr, Treppenhausbeleuchtung, Schornsteinreinigung.
Nicht zur Miete rechnen Umlagen für Zentralheizung, Warmwasserversorg., Garagenmiete, Untermieterzuschlag, Zuschlag für Möblierung.
volle DM
10 a) Handelt es sich um eine Dienst-, Werkswohnung, Berufs- oder Geschäftsmietwohnung? nein / ja
b) Ist die Wohnung verbilligt, kostenlos überlassen oder ist die Miete wegen finanzieller Vorleistungen (z. B. Mieterdarlehen) ermäßigt? nein / ja

FÜR LEERSTEHENDE WOHNUNGEN
11 Seit wie vielen Monaten steht die Wohnung leer? bis 3 / 4-6 / 7-12 / 13 oder mehr

Gebäudeangaben: Bitte nur ausfüllen, wenn Sie Eigentümer(in) oder Verwalter(in) dieses Gebäudes sind.
1 Gebäudeart *
Wohngebäude (Gebäude mindestens zur Hälfte für Wohnzwecke genutzt)
sonstiges Gebäude mit Wohnraum
bewohnte Unterkunft (z. B. Baracke)
Außerdem bei Wohnheimen:
Wird dieses Gebäude vollständig oder teilweise als Wohnheim genutzt? vollständig / teilweise
2 Wer ist Eigentümer(in), Kaufanwärt. bzw. Erbbauberechtigte(r) des Gebäudes?
Einzelperson oder Ehepaar, Erbengemeinschaft oder ähnliche Personengemeinschaft
Gemeinschaft von Wohnungseigentümern (nur bei Eigentumswohnungen)
gemeinnütziges Wohnungsunternehmen, Wohnungsbaugenossensch. oder Organ der staatl. Wohnungspolitik
freies Wohnungsunternehmen
sonstige(r) Eigentümer(in)
3 Baujahr des Gebäudes
(Jahr der Bezugsfertigstellung)
Bei Erweiterungs- und Umbauten ist das ursprüngliche Baujahr anzugeben, bei Wiederaufbau nach Totalschaden das Jahr des Wiederaufbaus.
bis 1900 / 1901-18 / 1919-48 / 1949-57 / 1958-62 / 63 / 64 / 65 / 66 / 67
68 / 69 / 70 / 71 / 72 / 73 / 74 / 75 / 76 / 77
78 / 79 / 80 / 81 / 82 / 83 / 84 / 85 / 86 / 87
4 Sind Wohnungen im Gebäude mit Mitteln des sozialen Wohnungsbaus gefördert? *
(nur Erster Förderungsweg)
keine / alle / nur ein Teil

VZ 87/7.86
Fläche (7) Miete (9) Gebäude
NUR VOM STATISTISCHEN LANDESAMT AUSZUFÜLLEN
0
* siehe Erläuterungen im Haushaltsmantelbogen

The "residential form" from the 1987 census in West Germany.

expertise."[10] Even a fleeting comparison of these two methods of data acquisition reveals the great cultural divide that I have been discussing all along. When the opponents of the census were up in arms about the "comprehensive registration of all the data concerning the population,"[11] and when demonstrators occupied all the public squares in Germany to rally against the "surveillance state," these protests in fact took place on the basis of a data set whose banality is almost laughable from today's perspective. Every new member on Facebook discloses far more information simply by creating a profile.

What happened in such a short time? How is it possible to explain this rapid and profound change in the way that people deal with registering their personal information? Today, "registration" is no longer perceived first and foremost as an act of victimization – as a show of force executed by authorities such as the "state" or the "police." For most people, on the contrary, it has become a productive activity. What had repulsed the opponents of the census – namely, the horrifying scenario of "surveillance" – has now been revived as a social virtue of "communication." Over the course of this transition, the concept of transparency has also undergone a complete shift in meaning. Instead of implying something threatening, transparency is now an expected feature of ethical behavior. There is no longer any talk at all about "people made of glass," for instance, though this and similar terms had been ubiquitous in the critical discourse of the 1980s. Today, the attribute of transparency is, instead, a sign of integrity.

The police as a catalyst of electronic registration

Measured by today's standards of data circulation, the resistance to the 1987 census looks almost pathological. The agitated voices yelling from podiums and the protest marches through the streets seem like quite hysterical reactions to the government's wish to know such things as the type of heating used in one's apartment or one's preferred means of public transportation. What was the source of all this outrage?

Interestingly enough, the opponents of the census did in fact discuss the pettiness of the survey questions. One critical article from 1987 pointed out, for instance, "the undeniable harmlessness of the individual census data." Even 30 years ago, that is, the nominal value of each individual piece of information was not a cause for concern; rather, the threat was thought to lie in the menacing potential of the data set as a whole. For, as noted in the same article, the triviality of the questions "conceals ... the explosive nature of their multifunctional correlative possibilities."[12] With computer-based registration, it would be possible to divide, filter, compare and recombine the data sets, and this uncontrollable proliferation was what the protesters really feared. They had no faith at all in the government's assurances that, in accordance with the fundamental right to "informational self-determination," severe restrictions would be put in place to limit the ways in which the data could be processed. The fact that the government guaranteed the anonymity of the information provided on the personal form and the residential form, for instance, was regarded by the resistance movement as an empty gesture. The reference numbers on the forms, according to the critics, "would make it possible to identify registered respondents at any time."[13]

In retrospect, this fear of registration, which seems so alien today, must have been related in some way to the media situation during the 1970s and 1980s. It was during these years that various administrative bodies began to collect formerly dispersed documents – such as files, index cards, forms and protocols – into electronic "databases," and this activity did not escape public attention. The integration of previously heterogeneous personal data, the purpose and potential applications of which were obscure, gave rise to a diffuse sense of concern. Thus, the censuses announced for 1983 and 1987 were simply especially prominent targets of an ongoing critique that had been aimed at various administrative transitions throughout these years. Around the same time as the 1987 census, for instance, similar resentments were being voiced about the creation of computer-readable ID cards and about the police sharing information with the Department of Motor Vehicles. The protesters against the census even managed to direct hostility toward the popularity of new media technologies such as cable television and teletext. In a piece of criticism bearing the dystopian title "Schöne neue Kabelwelt" ["Brave New Cable World"], for instance, Claus Fokke Wermann proclaimed: "Whoever participates is converted into data. Or, put another way, wherever there is teletext, there are data problems."[14] The editors of the anti-census book mentioned above ("What You Can Do Against the Micro-Census and the National Census") made a similar point with familiar diction: "In the age of cable television and teletext, consumer behavior can be monitored and controlled ... and the users of such technology can be manipulated in an effective and targeted manner."[15]

Why, exactly, did the concepts of "registration" and "datafication" have such negative connotations in the 1980s? What is immediately striking is how often the opponents of the census referred to the crimes of National Socialism. In 1983, the Second World War was hardly a distant memory, and thus the critical reception of the planned census made a point to emphasize the excessive use of registration by the Nazi government. In their book *The Nazi Census: Identification and Control in the Third Reich*, which was originally published in German in 1984, Götz Aly and Karl Heinz Roth analyzed the administrative conditions behind the Holocaust and openly associated their main thesis – namely, that optimized registration practices enabled the persecution and killing of the Jews – with the census planned for 1983. They posed the questions, for instance: "Is not the simple abstraction of humans into mere numbers a fundamental assault on their dignity? By profiling individuals, does the temptation not arise to regulate and, as statisticians like to put it, clean them up?"[16] And they understood these rhetorical questions both as a summary of their historical analysis and as an expression of solidarity with those protesting against the census at hand. Their main argument against censuses – that they "constitute an assault on the social imagination"[17] – could be made all the more forcefully because the authors, on account of their expertise as historians, knew where such measures could lead. For, as their research revealed, "The registration and bureaucratic isolation of the Jews in Germany began with the census of June 16, 1933."[18] In 1987, Götz Aly once again underscored the topicality of the Nazi administration to the unfolding situation by publishing a summary of his book in a brochure opposed to the forthcoming census.[19] In this context, the National Socialist state seemed to be an important point of reference because it demonstrated the latent dangers of unleashing the proposed methods of registration. The numerous evocations of the Third Reich served the same purpose in the work "What You Can Do Against the Micro-Census and the National Census." To its editors, censuses and indiscriminate data processing – which blur the boundaries between politics, the government and the police – had been characteristic features of the Nazi dictatorship. When the constitution of the Federal Republic of Germany was created, "it was unanimously agreed that such a condition would never be permitted to recur. All of this seems to have been forgotten."[20]

The crimes of National Socialism reverberated clearly in the West German protests against the censuses during the 1980s. However, because censuses had already been taken in 1950, 1956, 1961, and 1970 without any noteworthy resistance, this traumatic historical parallel could not have been  the primary impetus behind the rampant fear of registration. Something must have happened between 1970 and 1983 to have altered the perception of "datafication" and to have caused people to distrust registration processes. As mentioned above, the shift was related to the media-technical innovations of the time and their earliest areas of application.

In which contexts did computer-generated knowledge about human beings first emerge in the public sphere? Who were the individuals whose registration and identification first prompted the authorities to install such expensive and expansive electronic apparatuses? These questions must be kept in mind in order to understand why the disclosure of personal information had become such a sensitive issue. In 1968, Horst Herold, the newly appointed President of the Federal Criminal Police Office in West Germany, published an essay titled "Organisitorische Grundzüge der elektronischen Datenverarbeitung im Bereich der Polizei" ["Organizational Principles of Electronic Data-Processing in the Field of Police Work"), in which he stressed that "the activity of the police has always been that of generating, processing, evaluating and transferring data."[21] At that time, the West German police archives contained around 15 million files that did not communicate with one another, and for Herold this represented a scandalous fragmentation of data that made it difficult to fight crime in a productive manner. In his opinion, the future effectiveness of the police force depended on integrating all of these loose files as comprehensively as possible. This would require, as he put it, "a comprehensive survey of all data relating to crimes and criminals in a systematized and mechanized form."[22] With respect to solving crimes, that is, he believed the most important factor was neither the brilliant intuition of a detective nor the persistence of a good patrolman but rather the efficient processing of information. A criminologist with Marxist inclinations, Herold maintained that "mechanization will lead to police awareness."[23] Horst Herold's computer-based expansion of police manhunting methods and his central role in the struggle against the Red Army Faction are well documented, and so there is no need to go into the details here. For my purposes, it is crucial to underscore that, in West Germany, computer-based knowledge about individuals and the systems implemented to collect this information (such as the "Inpol" database, which was introduced in 1972) were associated from the very beginning with hunting down criminals. Registering people electronically was synonymous with optimizing police investigations and verifying suspicions. It was the police who decided whose data should be "stored," and the criteria for this decision were exceptionally broad because Herold's electronic manhunt focused not only on what people were doing but also on what they were *not* doing. As of the late 1970s, his groundbreaking innovation was to use computers to filter through lists of names and seemingly mundane personal information in order to identify perpetrators who lacked criminal records. Herold himself referred to this method as a "negative dragnet investigation," and its aim was to "reduce, by processes of elimination, the police dataset to a small remainder of potential suspects."[24] With this investigative method, however, all sorts of marginal information about any unobtrusive individual could possibly raise suspicion. It was an approach by the police that involved, much like the censuses under protest, the acquisition of large volumes of data by means of distributed surveys.

To its critics, the computerized census represented nothing less than "totalitarian forms of digitalization,"[25] and this fear was amplified in the middle of the 1980s by the seemingly prophetic representation of similar processes in works of literature. It seemed as though the most well-known dystopia in twentieth-century fiction, which had been written in the years after the Second World War, was about to become reality. George Orwell's *Nineteen Eighty-Four* is mentioned in just about every article and pamphlet that was written in support of the protest movement. Especially in the spring of 1983, the forthcoming census was regarded as a sign that the horrifying world imagined by Orwell was about to be realized right on schedule. "The census scheduled for April 27, 1983," according to one collection of oppositional essays, "is a timely catalyst for the fear and anger welling up in all of us about the actualization of Orwell's vision."[26] About the success of a pamphlet titled "Computer beherrschen das Land" ["Computers Will Rule the Country"], an article in the same volume declared: "Those who claim that we should fear the coming of an Orwellian surveillance state have hit the bulls-eye."[27] On the day after the Federal Constitutional Court had suspended the planned census, the main headline in the *Süddeutsche Zeitung*, a popular newspaper, was "Warten auf Orwells Jahr" ["Waiting for Orwell's Year"]. The literary representation of a totalitarian state in which "telescreens," mounted on every corner, constantly monitor the population served as a convenient model in the media's coverage of the 1983 census – and likewise in 1987, even though the novel's imagined year had passed, the book continued to be a popular reference. Writing on the eve of that census, two critics remarked: "What Orwell's novel *1984* warned us about – a world of totalitarian surveillance, a world of terror and bureaucracy, of administrative mendacity and manipulation ... this has become today's concrete reality."[28]

The semantics of the net

Throughout all of this, the fear of being registered was tied to anxieties about the imminent "networking" of information,[29] which, as far as the protesters were concerned, was the ultimate goal of the census at hand, and which had an accurate model in Orwell's fictitious state of Oceania. During the 1980s, the words "net," "network," and "networking" had unmistakably threatening overtones. The terms called to mind the expansion of a sophisticated and powerful authority whose sphere of influence was unclear. Beginning in 1979, the *Spiegel* magazine began to publish a long-running series of articles on "the path toward the surveillance state," and it is no coincidence that the catchphrase of the series was "The Steel Net Is Draping Over Us" ("Das Stahlnetz stülpt sich über uns").[30] Whoever got caught up in this sprawling web of computer-aided data acquisition – or so the message went – would face reduced freedoms and threats to their identity.

It is interesting that, in the popular imagination, the semantics of the "network" were still vaguely negative even during the early stages of the internet. The 1995 film *The Net*, for instance, revolved around the latent paranoid potential that exists in the relationship between individuals and electronic media. Played by Sandra Bullock, the main character is a software specialist named Angela Bennett whose social isolation increases as she spends more and more time online. The young woman no longer has any family connections (her dad abandoned the family long ago, and her senile mother is in a nursing home); she works at home in a jogging suit for a software company based in another city; her love life is restricted to bland online chats; and she even orders pizza on the internet, which in 1995 was not yet a sign of a mobile urban lifestyle but rather an acute indication of loneliness. A day before she is about to leave on a vacation (her "first in six years"), Bennett discovers a hoard of secret documents on one of her employer's computer disks and soon becomes the target of terrorist computer hackers who manipulate the stock market. The group has to recover the disk (mobile data storage like the "cloud" did not yet exist at the time), and when they struggle to do so, the hackers gradually begin to delete Bennett's identity in order to put pressure on her. All of her forms of identification have been stolen, and suddenly she is no longer registered at the beach hotel where she is staying in Mexico. When she goes to the consulate to request a visa, the officials there take her for another person, "Ruth Marx," and it is only under this name that she is allowed to return to the United States. Having flown back to California, she discovers that her car is no longer parked at the airport and that her house has been cleaned out and put up for sale by a woman named "Angela Bennett." The film plays through the thought-experiment of what an isolated person, whose existence is more or less confined to online worlds, can possibly do to prove who she really is. Angela Bennett, who is friendless and works from home, has just one personal connection in all of Los Angeles, namely with her former therapist, who thinks that the story about her swapped identity is utterly delusional. Her adversaries, who have access to police computers and hospital records, change her fingerprints and give her a criminal record. When Angela Bennett is finally arrested, her entire profile matches that of a fugitive named Ruth Marx. Even the public defender assigned to her case regards her account of events as pure paranoia.

Because *The Net* is a conventional Hollywood movie with a happy ending, the protagonist is able to clarify all of the confusion in the final minutes. She exposes the ring of cyberterrorists founded by her employer; the real Ruth Marx is found dead; and her own true identity is re-established. In terms of media history, however, the film is interesting because it shows that the idea of "networking" computer-generated data could still conjure up a great deal of anxiety in 1995, and because of its depiction of what will happen if people begin to immerse themselves online. Everything about the film's representation of the main character is meant to suggest that, by interacting with others exclusively through computers, a person will put his or her entire existence at stake. While sitting on the Mexican beach with her open laptop, the shy Angela Bennett is addressed for the first time by a member of the hacker cell: "Computers are your life, aren't they?" "Yes," she replies: "Perfect hiding place." Shortly after becoming a common component of everyday life, the internet was regarded as an *anti-social* network – the lives of vulnerable subjects could be destroyed by this web of data. "Our whole world is sitting there on a computer," Bennett explains to her lawyer (in terms that call to mind the brochures produced by the census protesters): "It's like this little electronic shadow on each and every one of us, just, just begging for someone to screw with."

The glamour of datafication

At the same time as movie-goers were able to watch Sandra Bullock struggle against her own demise, an entirely different notion of the electronic "net" was gaining ground. Far from regarding "registration" as something threatening, this latter interpretation rather associated it with the productive potential of data-driven identity. The first online dating sites were founded; the patent for the SixDegrees network was submitted; the books by Howard Rheingold, Nicholas Negroponte, and Sherry Turkle celebrated the liberating and self-determined nature of virtual communities; and the early European "net criticism" formulated by Geert Lovink, Pit Schultz, and others, though oppositional to those who praised unsullied "cyberspace" without restraint, still resembled the Californian internet pioneers to the extent that it likewise emphasized the active qualities of participating on the "net": "Net criticism, as Pit Schultz and I have defined it," claimed Lovink in 1996, "does not want to take the outsider's point of view. It positions itself within the Net, inside the software and wires."[31] During the dawning age of digital culture, the internet was no longer thought to produce sociophobic loners like Angela Bennett, but rather socially integrated citizens – engaged "netizens" (in the neologistic lingo of the late 1990s). While it may be true that, today, to be "networked" is no longer suggestive of external control but is rather understood as a performative act, as a communicative skill without which it would be impossible to have a career or a fulfilling social life, it should be kept in mind that these positive connotations are barely 20 years old. The "net" of electronically integrated data is no longer perceived as a threat to our existence; in both the market-oriented and critical rhetoric of digital culture, it is regarded instead as a catalyst and as a malleable piece of infrastructure. If anything, one could say that the discussions of "networks" and "registration" over the past 20 years have been characterized by their remarkable *lack* of paranoia.

The thoroughness of this transition becomes clear when one compares the deeply felt unease regarding methods of data circulation, which repeatedly came to the surface in

Germany during the 1980s, with today's standards of behavior. In 2011, an EU-wide census was taken (the first in Germany since 1987), and it did not incite any dissent. Everyday methods of self-datafication – in the form of social-media profiles, location services on smartphones, or mobile body measurements – have become so entrenched in society that the information requested by a census hardly seems to pose a threat. As mentioned above, proponents of the quantified-self movement consider measuring and counting to be formational aspects of their identity. If Fitbit's website can openly claim that the "Flex" wristband "tracks every part of your day,"[32] then ubiquitous registration is no longer a horrifying scenario but, rather, a public service.

This fundamental shift in collective mentality is undoubtedly related to the various types of entities that have demanded our registration. During the 1980s, it was the government whose requests for information, in the form of a census, engendered so much distrust in so many people. To be registered by the "state" was synonymous with forfeiting the autonomous core of one's own personality, converting human dignity into bar codes, or being "regulated" and "cleaned up," as Götz Aly and Karl Heinz Roth put it in 1984.[33] If one reads through the discreetly placed "privacy guidelines" of companies such as Facebook, Instagram, or Snapchat, which can only be discovered after a long series of clicks, it immediately becomes apparent that the information in one's profile is processed and disseminated in a number of ways that are not clearly explained. And yet the emotional response of those using social media (which is almost every single person in countries such as Germany and the United States) is the exact opposite of the registration phobia of the 1980s. To be converted into data by the global corporations of digital culture is typically not a cause of paranoia and anxiety – rather, it is associated with a sense of belonging. Here there is no risk of being caught in the cold tentacles of the state; it is really about being part of a community of users. In the history of media technology, perhaps no piece of foundational rhetoric has had a more lasting effect than the discourse about self-development and community formation during the early years of the internet – bromides that live on today in every keynote speech delivered by Mark Zuckerberg and in every cozy advertisement for Airbnb. The promise of being together with others via one's "timelines" and "stories" overshadows all of the ongoing transactions that take place between users and providers, even though the companies' business model of acquiring and sharing personal information can be understood as a refined and opaque version of the very governmental registration practices that had incited so much resistance during the 1980s.

It is just this sort of interrelational nexus that makes Michel Foucault's analyses – from his early concept of the "microphysics of power" to his observations about "governmentality" in his later lectures – so useful for understanding the human image in digital culture. For, given that his pioneering Marxist critique, with its clear division between suppressors and the suppressed, was meant above all to draw attention to the ubiquity and placelessness of power relations, then the comprehensive expansion of registration processes over the past quarter-century – from the intermittent censuses mandated by state authorities to the omnipresent data surveys on the internet – corroborate his theories in an unexpected way. After 1989, with the collapse of the socialist states and the end of the Cold War (events that were remarkably synchronized with the rise of digital culture), the traditional agents and instances of political power in Europe and North America lost a great deal of their former visibility. During the 1990s, this diminished position was also reflected in the notable decline in protest movements against the "state." At this same time, increasingly deregulated private corporations began to adopt the government's registration techniques and integrate them into digital communication technologies. These new relations no longer fit the understanding of power that fueled the political critique and the protest movements from 1968 until the end of the 1980s; it is no longer possible to draw a clear distinction between the suppressor and the suppressed, between the registering body and the registered. In the early 1990s, publications such as the magazine *Wired* helped to breed an unexpected alliance between internet activists, who came from the Californian counter-culture, and conservative liberal-market politics. These two spheres came together in their common desire to defend the establishment of digital infrastructures from government regulations.[34] The computer-aided registration of human beings has thus proliferated in many ways, but the social and political dynamics surrounding the circulation of personal information have taken shape in a way that was totally unforeseen.

Nineteen Eighty-Four from today's perspective

The extent to which the current situation differs from that of the 1980s becomes especially clear when one revisits the obligatory reference from that time – George Orwell's *Nineteen Eighty-Four* – from the perspective of today's media reality. Compared to the present day, it is amazing both how similar and how dissimilar Orwell's imagined world is. If, 30 years ago, the countless critics of the census who feared the imminent arrival of the fictitious "surveillance state" could have known about all of the technological developments to come, they certainly would have felt as though their fears were justified. For, in the early twenty-first century, the presence of networked screens in every apartment, in every subway station, and on every street corner reached a degree of density never achieved in Orwell's post-apocalyptic and war-torn Oceania. "The telescreen received and transmitted simultaneously,"[35] the novel informs us about the monitoring devices installed all across London. News, instructions, and motivational songs from the Party are broadcast into every apartment "from an oblong metal plaque like a dulled mirror which formed part of the surface of the right-hand wall."[36] This instrument, the narrator explains, "could be dimmed, but there was no way of shutting it off completely."[37] In *Nineteen Eighty-Four*, every human movement is recorded by the displays – "Whichever way you turned, the telescreen faced you"[38] – and this total surveillance is coupled with the government's insistence on constant social interaction. "It was assumed," writes Orwell about the expectations of a Party member, "that when he was not working, eating or sleeping he would be taking part in some kind of communal recreation: to do anything that suggested a taste for solitude, even to go for a walk by yourself, was always slightly dangerous."[39] Unrecorded activity raises suspicion, and a "taste for solitude" is regarded as a latent pathology: in the debates from 2012 about potential mass murderers and their supposed preference to abstain from Facebook, this imperative to socialize looks awfully familiar.

In light of the present state of media technology, it is safe to say that Orwell was quite prophetic (though he was a few decades off the mark), and it is telling that sales of *Nineteen Eighty-Four* tend to spike during times of political crisis, as they did after the election of Donald Trump at the end of 2016. Taken on their own, however, these occasional similarities are not very significant. Of far greater interest are the fundamental differences that exist between the political context of the novel's dystopian world and the circumstances today. Today, almost everyone in North America and Europe lives in a free and democratic state (recent political developments notwithstanding). There is no totalitarian surveillance regime controlling the activities and thoughts of its subjects and punishing every transgression with drastic measures. Instead of the tyrannical state envisioned by Orwell, the center of data circulation in today's media reality is composed of an array of discrete providers: a series of publicly traded global corporations that are not perceived as being oppressive even though they presumably possess more information about people than any secret service ever could.[40]

In *Nineteen Eighty-Four*, the seats of power are visible at all times and can be located with precision. The gigantic buildings that house the "Ministries," which resemble those of National Socialism, loom over the city of London: "So completely did they dwarf the surrounding architecture that from the roof of Victory Mansions you could see all four of them simultaneously. They were the homes of the four Ministries between which the entire apparatus of government was divided."[41] The personnel structure of this apparatus is a system of concentric circles, with "Big Brother" in the center, then a close ring consisting of the elite members of the "Inner Party," who have access to the telescreens, and finally the marginal and oppressed bulk of the population – the so-called "Outer Party" to which the novel's protagonist, Winston Smith, belongs. Within this hierarchical system, the use of electronic media is only conceivable as a measure of control wielded by the state authorities: "With the development of television, and the technical advance which made it possible to receive and transmit simultaneously on the same instrument," the narrator explains, "private life came to an end. Every citizen, or at least every citizen important enough to be worth watching, could be kept for twenty-four hours a day under the eyes of the police and in the sound of official propaganda."[42] Registration, recording, and police investigations are one and the same in Orwell's novel, and this conflation results in a human image of total uniformity. For, as soon as the system of telescreens was put in place, "The possibility of enforcing not only complete obedience to the will of the State, but complete uniformity of opinion on all subjects, now existed for the first time."[43]

The surveillance regime in *Nineteen Eighty-Four* is intended to eliminate any and all sorts of individual development. Oceania is inhabited by "[t]hree hundred million people all with the same face."[44] They all eat the same cabbage soup, wear the same jacket, are awakened at the same time every morning by the telescreen, and occupy the same prescribed world of thought. In his novel, Orwell depicted a sort of fascist or Stalinist totalitarianism that has been optimized by way of media technology. Yet this horrifying vision, which seemed plausible in the aftermath of the Second World War (and still resonated in the 1980s), never came to pass. Today, ubiquitous registration is no longer perceived as something coercive but is rather a voluntary aspect of the new media reality; the decree of uniformity has been replaced by an insistence on individual self-development. Whereas the telescreens in *Nineteen Eighty-Four*, which are "delicate enough" to register a person's heartbeat,[45] do so in the name of control, today's wearables and smart watches, which perform the same task, are used to satisfy a collective desire for self-quantification. The emblem of datafied life in Orwell's novel is the pallid and subdued Party member who is worn down by constant surveillance. Who would Winston Smith be in today's digital culture? The young man in the café taking selfies in the now-familiar pose and quickly posting these pictures on Instagram to provide his followers with new images? The man jogging in the park, with a tracking device in his shoe and a Fitbit around his wrist, who plans to upload his step count and heart rate for the whole community to see?

Instead of smothering our identities, today's processes of datafication define their shape and representation. In Orwell's novel, one of the tactics of the despotic regime is to deprive people of their personal memories. Keeping a diary, for instance, is an offence punishable by death. Without being able to call to mind your own biography, as the narrator says about Winston Smith, "even the outline of your own life lost its sharpness."[46] For Smith, the act of circumventing this memory ban and writing down his own impressions is a form of inner resistance, as are his rendezvous with his lover Julia. Because Party members are only permitted to procreate by means of artificial insemination, sexual desire is regarded as a "Thoughtcrime" in Oceania. Ultimately, sex is a form of protest: "Their embrace had been a battle, the climax a victory. It was a blow struck against the Party. It was a political act."[47] This fusion of sexual and political liberation surely contributed to the novel's success after 1968. At its core, subversion in Orwell's work means finding refuge from telescreens and microphones. According to the ethics of the novel, the sphere of humanity is unrecordable and unrecorded. After a (presumably) furtive tryst with Julia, Winston emphatically declares: "They can't get inside you. If you can *feel* that staying human is worthwhile, even when it can't have any result whatever, you've beaten them."[48] Referring to the Party's informers, the narrator adds: "They could lay bare in the utmost detail everything that you had done or said or thought; but the inner heart, whose workings were mysterious even to yourself, remained impregnable."[49] Individuals are only able to preserve their human dignity in areas beyond the reach of electronic data acquisition – a credo or axiom of humanity that the opponents of the West German census would adopt 35 years later. Such opposition has dissipated in the far-reaching agendas of today's digital culture. Today, human beings are chiefly defined by the extent to which they convert themselves into data and communicate this information via digital media. The ego has become a profile.

Meanwhile, the formerly horrifying world depicted in *Nineteen Eighty-Four* has become nothing more than an ironic reference in 21st-century popular culture. *Big Brother*, which debuted in the Netherlands in 1999 and became an international franchise the following year, is a surveillance show that still entices tens of thousands of auditions for every new season (even though the popularity of the program has waned to such an extent that its contestants seem to sit around attracting as much attention as Kafka's hunger artist). Another reference to Orwell concerns his portrayal, toward the end of *Nineteen Eighty-Four*, of the Party's torture practices in Room 101 of the "Ministry of Love," which everyone in Oceania fears and which Winston Smith himself has to experience after his denunciation. "The thing that is in Room 101 is the worst thing in the world," says O'Brien, the mysterious Party official, as he leads Winston into the torture chamber: "The worst thing in the world," he goes on, "varies from individual to individual. It may be burial alive, or death by fire, or by drowning, or by impalement, or fifty other deaths. There are cases where it is some quite trivial thing, not even fatal."[50] A guard enters the room carrying "a box or basket of some kind," and begins to prepare Winston's torture session:

> It was an oblong wire cage with a handle on top for carrying it by. Fixed to the front of it was something that looked like a fencing mask, with the concave side outwards. Although it was three or four metres away from him, he could see that the cage was divided lengthways into two compartments, and that there was some kind of creature in each. They were rats.... "You can't do that!" he cried out in a high cracked voice. "You couldn't, you couldn't! It's impossible."[51]

O'Brien begins to set the torture process in motion; he fastens the delinquent to his chair and places a mask over his head that is attached to a cage full of rats, which are now separated from Winston's head by two partitions. He then lifts the first partition: "Again the black panic took hold of him. He was blind, helpless, mindless."[52] It is unknown whether the creator of the popular television program *I'm a Celebrity ... Get Me Out of Here!* had been familiar with this scene from *Nineteen Eighty-Four* when he came up with the show's so-called "Bushtucker Trials," in which the heads or entire bodies of the contestants are placed in glass boxes which are in turn filled with rats, mice, or insects. The similarity of the design is uncanny, and whereas Winston is able to save himself at the last second from actually coming into contact with the rats by betraying his lover Julia, the celebrities in the jungle endure the challenge and proudly return to camp with the "stars" that they have earned for their suffering (these can be exchanged for more appetizing food and drink on the show). In *Nineteen Eighty-Four*, as the character O'Brien says, this sort of mechanism produces the same amount of fear as potentially burning to death, drowning, or being impaled, and although Winston Smith survives the procedure physically, it completely breaks his will to be free and extinguishes his inner life. The viewers of *I'm a Celebrity*, in contrast, regard the image of rats scrambling over someone's encased head as something routine, and the journalists who write about trashy television nonchalantly discuss whether this year's season is more entertaining than those of the past.

Stigmatization and self-design

In multiple ways today, previously despotic forms of empowerment function as means of expressing subjectivity – a transition that each of the chapters of this book has illustrated with various examples. Formerly a disciplinary instrument, the profile has emerged as a method of self-representation. The use of technology to locate individuals, which just ten years ago was primarily restricted to the contexts of law enforcement and criminal justice, is now an essential precondition for social transactions, popular games, and finding a romantic partner. Finally, measuring the body, which in the human sciences was likewise motivated by the desire to register deviant subjects, now promises in the form of wearables and health apps to contribute to our sovereign and self-determined existence. All of these methods of self-tracking have stripped the practice of registration, which prompted collective protests just 30 years ago, of its menacing connotations. No longer is it an authoritarian and opaque authority that collects data about the lives, locations, and bodies of individual people; the registering authority and the registered have rather melded into one, and they enhance the so-called "liquid surveillance" that Zygmunt Bauman and David Lyon have recently identified as a major feature of digital culture.[53]

Of course, digital culture allows us to make our own decisions. The circumstances are not those of a fictional or actual dystopian or authoritarian regime. No one is forced to create a social-media profile, use location-based services on their phone, or even to own a smartphone at all (even though the refusal to do so would result in being excluded from more and more spheres of communication and activity). As the initiatives of digital activists have shown, it is also possible to enjoy the perks of the latest media technologies while remaining vigilant against the registration, identification, and location techniques employed by large corporations. Finn Brunton and Helen Nissenbaum's 2015 book *Obfuscation*, for instance, offers excellent tips on how to obscure one's personal information.[54] That said, the fundamental shifts that have taken place over the last 25 years in the relationship between subject-formation and registration techniques have caused these alternative options to fade into the background. Even Edward Snowden's revelations from 2013, which clearly showed that today's governments have access to previously unthinkable amounts of their citizens' personal information, incited no more than a brief stint of public outrage. This eye-opening knowledge simply cannot compete with the universal narratives of "sharing" and being "social." It is one of the paradoxes of digital culture that, in an era when such large amounts of personal data are being controlled by outside entities, the rhetoric of self-determination is flourishing more than ever.

This gesture of autonomy, moreover, has not been restricted to data-driven forms of subject-formation – it pertains just as well to the immediately physical phenomenon of the human body. As with the development of the profile format in digital culture, over the past 20 years the presentation of one's own body – in particular, one's own skin – has been influenced by a technique that was once used to stigmatize individuals. Of course, I am referring here to the astounding popularity of tattoos. As recently as 1984, the following remarks could be found in a reference work for police: "Tattoos are common among sailors, soldiers, workers, and prisoners. In port cities, there are often special tattoo parlors.... From the perspective of criminology, tattoos are of interest above all as identifying features in personal descriptions. Moreover, they often reveal things about the origin and social environment of those who have them."[55]

Various functions have been attributed to tattoos throughout the history of law enforcement. Up until the late eighteenth century in Europe, in fact, having a tattoo was equivalent to being stigmatized; convicted criminals were given a mark of shame, such as the flower tattooed on Milady de Winter's shoulder in Dumas's novel *The Three Musketeers*. This form of punishment came to an end in the decades around the year 1800. The tattooed criminal body, however, gained renewed significance with the rise of criminal anthropology during the middle of the nineteenth century. At this point, they were no longer relevant as stigmatizing symbols imposed by the authorities but rather as potential clues to a criminal's motives. Cesare Lombroso, who while working as a prison doctor during the 1870s, supposedly studied the tattoos of more than 7,000 inmates,[56] discusses them again and again within his intricate classification system. He associated particular patterns with particular criminal types, and he attributed the commonness of tattoos among criminals to their greater tolerance of pain and to the general tedium of prison life. Hans Gross added to this discussion in his *Criminal Investigation: A Practical Handbook*. It was not necessary, he thought, to "go as far as" Lombroso and his followers, who considered "tattooing the characteristic sign of habitual criminals."[57] Nevertheless, he agreed with the criminal-anthropological school in his belief that "Tattooing will generally be met with among people of an energetic disposition: ... soldiers, sailors, butchers, fishermen, woodcutters, smiths, etc." He believed that the reason for this proclivity was not their high threshold for pain but rather their heightened "sexual sensitivity": "[I]t is for this reason that among persons of the feminine sex tattooing is in Europe generally only found among prostitutes."[58] As regards criminology, this meant that tattoos were more common among criminals of a similarly energetic sort, "such as murderers, hooligans, house-breakers, etc., and on the other hand among people of a sensual nature such as bullies, sodomites, ravishers, and others who commit crimes against morality, but not among cheats and thieves."[59]

By the end of the nineteenth century, the notion of the tattoo as a violently applied mark of shame had long been rejected. Alphonse Bertillon dismissed the question of why his anthropometric system did not include such a category with the following words: "Treating tattoos as a sign of criminality would be a covert reintroduction of stigmatization, and I strongly object to such an imposition."[60] With the glaring exception of tattooing inmate numbers on the prisoners at Auschwitz, this practice was otherwise never revived in the twentieth century. Nevertheless, police investigators maintained an interest in what tattoos might reveal about criminal motives, as is evident from the 1984 reference work cited above. That article had been written toward the end of an era in which tattoos could still be treated as stigmatizations with classificatory significance. Just a few years later, the third epoch in the European history of tattoos began to take its course, and this involved their transition from signs saturated in meaning to purely aesthetic elements of self-design. Now it is no longer the criminal or prostitute, the pederast or rapist, whose skin is covered in ink; rather, tattoos can be found on anyone and in every location: the secretary at the office, the professional athlete at the stadium, the family man at the public pool. Over the past few decades, tattoos have been purely decorative; they are no longer indicative of someone's deviant background, and they certainly do not "reveal things about the origin and social environment of those who have them," as they still did some 30 years ago.

In certain contexts, however, tattoos are still used to define identities and signify that someone belongs to one group or another. Since the middle of the 1990s, for instance, Nike has encouraged employees at its flagship stores to have the "swoosh" logo tattooed somewhere visible on their bodies – not under coercion, and not as a job requirement, but simply as a symbol of their identification with the brand.[61] This request – this "covert reintroduction of stigmatization," as Bertillon put it – illustrates the transformation that this book has attempted to delineate all along: formerly coercive methods of registration have become voluntary methods of self-styling; the constrictive procedures of the police and the criminal justice system have been refashioned into the free and cheerful tools of marketing.

5
The Power of Internalization

Everything that has been said in the preceding pages about the origins of digital culture's techniques for self-representation and self-perception could be distilled into a single word: unlike the profiled, located, and measured criminals and patients in the nineteenth and twentieth centuries, today's users of social media, location-based services, or wearables do so *voluntarily*. Yet what, exactly, does the category of "voluntariness" mean for the present status of subjectivity? Should the decisions made and the measures taken of one's own volition be understood as emancipatory acts against prescribed and enforced manners of behavior? Or, in these cases, does "voluntariness" imply instead an ongoing process of problematizing the self?

Without a doubt, one of the more striking features of the present is that many processes of normalizing and regulating people, which just a few decades ago had been the mandate of state, scientific, or police authorities, have been handed over to individuals. This development is evident not only with respect to the circulation of personal information but in other contexts as well. In the field of reproductive medicine, for instance, methods of prenatal and preimplantation screenings, which make it possible to test young embryos for irregularities or genetic defects, have resulted in the fact that hardly any children are born any more with complications such as

Down syndrome or cystic fibrosis. In this manner, the free and individual decision of the couple to follow the recommendations of doctors and geneticists fulfills a eugenically motivated agenda that had existed in authoritarian states during the first half of the twentieth century. In 1895, Alfred Ploetz, one of the founders of "racial hygiene" in Germany, recommended the "eradication of newborns" in order to elevate the collective genetic stock to a eugenically desirable level. During the "Third Reich," as is well known, these ideas were used to legitimate the government's health policy. Today, this same sort of eradication is carried out in a discreet and efficient manner during the earliest stages of a future person's existence, either in the mother's womb or even before a fetus is implanted in the birth mother. The motivations behind these two practices may be fundamentally different – one is concerned with the genetic material of an entire population, the other with a single family's personal happiness – but their consequences remain the same. Both Ploetz's proposal to "prepare, with a small dose of morphine, a gentle death for weak or malformed children"[1] and the aims of prenatal or preimplantation screening assert that life should be denied to human beings with flawed genetic constitutions.[2]

Over the last few decades, interventions undertaken at the end of human existence have shifted much like those employed at its beginning. Around the same time that "racial hygiene" became established in Germany, a debate was under way about "allowing the destruction of life unworthy of life," which was sparked by Karl Binding and Alfred Hoche's 1920 book with that title. There the lawyer and the psychiatrist recommended, for economic and demographic reasons, the systematic killing of so-called "ballast lives" – a label that the authors applied to terminally ill, comatose, and mentally disabled people.[3] This was exactly the sort of "euthanasia," in fact, that would be implemented without restraint by the Nazi regime. Since the Second World War, of course, the connection between caring for a nation's population and killing the sick with medical assistance has been discredited. Over the last 25 years, however, the readiness in Germany to assist the death of people suffering from certain conditions has been revived, even though this issue was absolutely taboo from the 1950s to the 1980s. Carried out in the name of the "will of the patient," this practice has been restricted to terminally ill individuals, just as the methods of prenatal and preimplantation screening have been used to benefit individual families. The binding nature of "living wills" or "advance healthcare directives" has been legally established since 2009; since then, euthanasia and the removal of life-support systems in the case of unresponsive patients have been permitted. For more than a decade, active forms of assisted suicide have been discussed by those interested in reformulating Germany's euthanasia laws. Those in favor of liberalizing the law evoke the individual right to a "dignified" death – self-determined, and without having to suffer senility or live in a nursing home. The previous sovereignty of the state to eradicate economically worthless life has thus given way to the sovereignty of the subject to end his or her own life with the help of medical assistance. The question remains, however, whether this development should be understood as a categorical change or as part of a continuum. Both models, after all, allow for the abolishment of lives that are supposedly no longer worth living.

What the biological sciences have presented as a transition from demographic and political interventions to the individual's freedom of choice – a tendency shared during the second half of the twentieth century by the field of genetics, which reoriented itself from a science concerned with populations to one concerned with individuals – applies just as well to the technologies of the self that I have described in this book. Up until the late twentieth century, technical limitations and problems of legitimation ensured that the generation of data about individual people – about their biographies, locations, and states of health – was restricted to the police and to scientific authorities dealing with exceptional circumstances. An individual would not become the object of registration unless a manhunt, an investigation, or his or her medical case history justified the costs and legal efforts involved. And the resistance to the first collective registration measures of the computer age, such as the censuses of 1983 and 1987, arose from the concern that the electronic storage of personal data would be equivalent to fabricating charges of wrongdoing.

Under the conditions of present-day media technology, the acquisition and dissemination of personal data do not need to be justified by a crisis scenario. On the one hand, people leave behind traces of their identity and location whenever they use a credit card or search for things online; on the other hand, a general appetite for self-registration, self-location, and self-measuring has developed that resembles the biopolitical tendency toward self-eugenics. But what, exactly, do these inclinations say about the disposition of the present? What functions and effects are associated with voluntarily taking over such regulatory processes? According to their most influential theorists, two major epochs can be identified in the history of modern power techniques. Michel Foucault spoke about the "disciplinary power" that, as of the eighteenth century, enclosed and organized individuals within the spaces of newly established institutions such as schools, barracks, factories, hospitals, and prisons. As Gilles Deleuze remarked in his famous essay "Postscript on the Societies of Control," the epoch of disciplinary power gradually dissipated over the course of the twentieth century. "We are in a generalized crisis in relation to all the environments of enclosure," he writes, noting that "ultrarapid forms of free-floating control" have replaced former disciplinary spaces – flexible and open "corporations" have taken the place of factories, while "perpetual training" seems to be replacing schools.[4] Yet this perceptive essay, which is now more than 25 years old, had been written before a new human image was shaped by digital culture and the biological and neurological sciences. Deleuze's imagined scenario is defined by hegemonic gestures and top-down hierarchies, as is clear from his following remarks: "The conception of a control mechanism, giving the position of any element within an open environment at any given instant (whether animal in a reserve or human in a corporation, as with an electronic collar), is not necessarily one of science fiction."[5] Perhaps it is true that, in the late twentieth century, prisons and factories with punch cards were no longer necessary to regulate deviant and subordinate people, but even the mobile control mechanisms of the time – as the example of the electronic ankle bracelet makes clear – were instruments of coercion and authority.

The electronic collar of the present, in contrast, is a product of the wearables industry, a wristband or a smart watch made by a company like Fitbit, which has adopted the following creed: "We believe you're more likely to reach your goals if you're encouraged to have fun, smile, and feel empowered along the way."[6] Moreover, the insurance company Generali describes the "philosophy" behind its new "Vitality" program, which is organized around collecting data from fitness wristbands, with these words: "This is what's important to us: working together to inspire you to lead a more active life and to eat more health-consciously – without any pressure at all and simply because it's what you want to do."[7] Past the disciplinary power of the eighteenth and nineteenth centuries, and beyond even the control power of the twentieth, the trajectory since the turn of the twenty-first century seems to have led to a third form of authority that could be called preventative power or the power of internalization. It ensures that data registries and conceptions of normal life no longer have to be established by external authorities but are, rather, collectively internalized. Create a profile! Share your own location! Become transparent! Dispose of disabled children! Commands such as these, which were once issued by authorities, are now desires that people satisfy without a second thought.

Competitive individuality

Our general readiness to be visible and quantifiable at all times has spawned forms of self-presentation that resemble product promotions. That the principles of criminological registration have been adopted by the field of marketing was already made clear in my discussion of the profile concept: methods developed by the FBI at the end of the 1970s to identify criminals are now being used today to identify consumers. It is characteristic of digital culture, however, that these methods are not only being applied by companies or advertising agencies in order to entice potential customers. They are also being implemented by individuals to market themselves. Users of social media, as Zygmunt Bauman has observed, "are simultaneously promoters of commodities and the commodities they promote."[8] Up until 25 years ago, it was hardly even possible to play both of these roles at once. For the great majority of people, as I mentioned at the beginning of this book, there was simply no platform for representing oneself to the public, and the creators of cultural goods who wanted to be in the public eye typically outsourced the advertisement of themselves and their products to others. The new media system has caused this division of labor to disappear. Almost every author, filmmaker, and musician today who puts out something new will wage a personal marketing campaign on his or her profile and inundate friends and followers with product references during the weeks before the release. To refuse to do so and to insist on the separation of artistic creation and PR work has become an exotic position.

The marketing-strategic approach to one's own self no longer creates a rift in the contemporary human image. Georg Lukács's diagnosis of the "reification" of social relations, which was central to the political and economic critique during the second half of the twentieth century, has become an enigmatic category under today's conditions.[9] Even in the census rulings issued by the Federal Constitutional Court, traces of Lukács's concept are recognizable in the prohibition against "forcefully registering people in their entire personality ... and thus treating them like an object," and in the constitutional directive stating that "an 'inner space' must be preserved for the sake of the free and self-determined development of an individual's personality."[10] In digital culture, this connection between "free development" and a protected "inner space" no longer exists; the development of the self is rather dependent on permanent media representations. One's own person is understood as a publicly circulating simulacrum whose attractiveness and value have to be confirmed and reinforced in a continuous process.

This activity has become so ingrained that forms of evaluation and rating are now second-nature in current modes of communication. On YouTube, young gamers regularly conclude videos of themselves with comments such as "If you like the content, hit the like button." Few people are unfamiliar with the hopeful impulse to check in on their own social media postings every few minutes to see whether the number next to the thumbs-up and heart icons has increased.

Yet this general imperative to evaluate things characterizes more than just our manners of speech and behavior; it has also been integrated into the mechanical operations of programs and services as a necessary component of daily transactions. In the case of Uber, for instance, no transaction is complete until the driver has been given a rating between one and five stars – thus, it is no longer a personal decision to evaluate another person but, rather, a technical default setting.

In a compelling book about downward economic mobility in Germany, the sociologist Oliver Nachtwey has recently discussed the "competitive individuality" that pervades the present: "It is a signature of our time," he observes, "that market and competitive mechanisms are implemented in nearly all spheres of society."[11] The incessant opportunities for evaluation during social interactions are a clear example of this. The proliferation of this phenomenon is also evident in the talent shows that are on television today (much like the playful reinterpretation of the formerly genuine anxieties surrounding registration). Ever since *Big Brother* and *Popstars* debuted in 2000, dramatic and artificially protracted decisions about which contestants should be kicked off a given show have become a familiar ritual. Heidi Klum, as is well known, relishes in drawing out this selection process in her program *Germany's Next Topmodel* by tormenting the candidates with misleading insinuations about which of them has failed to make the cut; the obligatory close-up shots focusing on the tears of the rejected girls are the climax of every episode. Today, such decision processes are a common feature of countless reality shows, and this surplus of repetitive drama has numbed us to the fact that staged competitive situations of this sort are still a relatively recent phenomenon. Competitions like this were not a part of television entertainment until the late 1990s, and it is telling that their appearance coincided perfectly with the emergence of surveillance shows. *Expedition Robinson* and *Big Brother* were the first programs in which groups of contestants were both relentlessly observed by the camera and gradually whittled down by an internal voting system. Total surveillance and internal competition – two categories that had once been fundamentally distinct – were united in these tense moments of television history as though they had always belonged together.

This casual synthesis, however, makes it doubly apparent that the source of collective anxiety shifted around the turn of the twenty-first century. Unchecked surveillance by external authorities is no longer a cause of dread. The contestants on these programs have no qualms at all about the hidden cameras and microphones surrounding them – in fact, they welcome their presence. What causes panic, in contrast, is the idea of losing a competition, earning negative evaluations, and being "voted off." In this respect, these television shows revolve around the same screening procedures as those used in every one of today's employment assessment centers.

The willingness to market oneself is therefore not a consequence of new media technology alone. Although this readiness has been enhanced by new technological formats, over the past 25 years the seemingly incessant need to be assessed has had just as much to do with economic conditions – with the immense structural changes that have been taking place since the 1980s in corporations and the job market in Western Europe and North America. With Germany as his example, Oliver Nachtwey has analyzed in detail the constant pressure faced by people whose professional careers consist of a fragile chain of temporary contracts. In his study, he defines the figure of the "self-employed employee" or "entreployee" – someone working intermittently within one project-based corporate structure or another – as the "model of modern subjectivity,"[12] much as Nikolas Rose and Ulrich Bröckling had used the concept of the "entrepreneurial self" to describe similar circumstances a few years earlier. Evaluation and self-representation are unavoidable facts of life for project collaborators whose employment status is always probationary: "Modern capitalism," according to Nachtwey, "does not function without collaboration, without the voluntary participation of individuals."[13] The fact that, since the 1990s, career advisers have been focusing so heavily on the "profiles" of job candidates should be understood in this very context (I discussed this phenomenon in the first chapter). The profile, as I see it, is the undeniable nodal point of "competitive individuality." To the extent that permanent jobs have been replaced by short-term and project-based contract positions, it has become all the more necessary to maintain a carefully cultivated profile in order to tip the balance in one's favor during the next round of applications – that is, during the next competition. (In the world of academia, for instance, this mentality is now par for the course. Ever since tenured professorships or long-term research positions became the exception instead of the norm, part-time or limited-term academics have had to dedicate more and more energy to perfecting their "research profiles" for future applications. Recording one's own accomplishments, which previous generations of scholars regarded as a burdensome administrative chore, has become a primary activity for those under constant evaluation and in constant need of recommendations. Maintaining a research profile now requires nearly as much attention as the research itself.)

The governability of the self in digital culture

Mechanisms of internalization are at work whenever people form ideas about "normal" life by means of self-tracking, and whenever they take over the role of external registering authorities by cultivating their own "profiles." Although these methods can strengthen the autonomy of the subject by emancipating him or her from intermediary authorities, they also contribute to the growing need to fulfill regulatory requirements. At the heart of this necessity are two sets of ideas that operate on the threshold between the present and the future: "risk" and "precaution." The reason why so many people wear a fitness wristband, check their heart rate on smartphones, purchase "behavior-based" life-insurance policies, or have their own genome tested for potential genetic diseases is to minimize their future health risks by exercising precaution. A social consensus has formed about the urgent importance of preventative measures for our safety and well-being. Oddly enough, this trend is in stark contrast to the growing acceptance of deviance that now defines the aesthetic realm. No one will bat an eye if a colleague shows up at work with a red mohawk and an arm covered in tattoos, but heads will shake and criticism will be voiced if someone rides a bike without a helmet, smokes cigarettes throughout the day, or neglects to be screened for colon cancer at the age of 45. A mere 25 years ago, exactly the opposite attitude prevailed.

In the human sciences, pioneering ideas about prevention happened to come from the very fields that played a prominent role in the history of measuring techniques. At the beginning of the twentieth century, Hugo Münsterberg remarked that thinking about "prevention" was a central aspect of psychotechnics.[14] In his introduction to behaviorism published in 1925, John Watson stated: "It is the business of behavioristic psychology to be able to predict and control human activity. To do this it must gather scientific data by experimental methods. Only then can the trained behaviorist predict, given the stimulus, what reaction will take place."[15] In the 1940s, this sort of analysis would be adopted by the new field of cybernetics and refined for military purposes.[16] In the field of criminology, electronic data processing was likewise embraced in the name of prevention. As early as 1968, Horst Herold referred to crime prevention as "the most important yet most neglected means of fighting crime."[17] More than just a tool for comparing information, data processing as he envisioned it would contribute above all to the systematic prevention of future criminal acts.

In today's digital culture, these cybernetic and criminological approaches to prevention go by the terms "micro-profiling" and "predictive analytics." The belief is that the electronic analysis of large data sets should make it possible to predict crimes in certain areas of a city and within certain sectors of the population. With this alleged knowledge of the future, preventative measures can then be put in place – such as an increased police presence – and manhunts can be initiated in advance of any wrongdoing. In this respect, preventative knowledge serves to enhance the control that authorities can exert over individuals, just as Münsterberg, Watson, or Herold had hoped all along. Regarding the current status of subjectivity, however, it is crucial to stress that these same preventative measures are being voluntarily implemented by individuals as control mechanisms over themselves. The racial profiling practiced by the police at train stations and on public transportation, which places individuals with certain ethnic features under stricter surveillance on account of predictive suspicion, is reflected in the self-made profiles of those networking on LinkedIn, while the GPS tracker placed around the ankle of someone on parole is reflected in the fitness bands worn by self-trackers. The interaction between "techniques of domination and techniques of the self," which Michel Foucault emphasized in his lectures on the art of government, is therefore vividly present in digital culture.[18] "The contact point," Foucault observed, "where the way individuals are driven by others is tied to the way they conduct themselves is what we can call, I think, government."[19] According to Ulrich Bröckling and his co-authors, this has the following implications for the "governmentality" of the present: "Government is not related first and foremost to the suppression of subjectivity but above all to its '(self-)production' or, to be more precise, to the creation and promotion of technologies of the self that can be tied to the government's goals."[20]

Profiles, location-based services, and measuring practices are paradigmatic elements of this promotion. They stabilize a political constellation that accommodates totalitarian methods of registration (according to Orwell's standards and those of his readers in the 1970s and 1980s) and yet is even more problematic because it is difficult to escape and thus difficult to critique. However inconsequential it might be, the one consolation in the novel *Nineteen Eighty-Four* was that it presented, from the perspective of both the characters and its conventional narrative, a clear dividing line between despotism and freedom, mendacity and the truth. The authorial narrator describes the infrastructures of state power from a distance; he is not caught up in its labyrinth, and this external position allows him space for reason and critique. Moreover, the large class of so-called "proles" in the novel, who live without rights or obligations but constitute 85 percent of Oceania's population, are illustrative of the (often overlooked) fact that the overwhelming majority of people in *Nineteen Eighty-Four* are not burdened by any state oversight at all. There are no telescreens watching over them in their apartments. If there is any remaining hope for humanity in Orwell's dystopia, it lies in this segment of society: "The proles had stayed human.... If there was hope, it lay in the proles!"[21] What, in today's digital culture, is analogous to these outsider positions? It is evident that refuges of this sort, which even Orwell's horrifying vision allowed to exist, are far more difficult to locate and personalize today. With regard to media technology, the area beyond the reach of registration has diminished to the extent that the general desire for self-datafication has grown. At least since 1989, the category of "class" has played a subordinate role in social, economic, and political debates, and this is largely because the prominent discourse about personal motivation – about everyone's "passion" to make his or her own success story come true – has pushed the realities of class distinction and the notion of class solidarity into the background.[22] The despotic surveillance state, which, 35 years ago, many people in West Germany feared was looming, never came to be. That said, the place and effectiveness of critique have undoubtedly eroded in today's "liquid modernity." In 1983 and 1987, the opponents of the census were able to attack the office buildings where all of the surveys were kept. It is not possible to throw bombs at the cloud.

During the last quarter of the twentieth century, what forces were responsible for this internalization of regulatory processes? In his recent book on what he calls the "society of singularities," the sociologist Andreas Reckwitz has drawn attention to the fact that, over the past 25 years, "the technological complex of computers, digitality, and the internet has led to the ongoing fabrication of subjects, objects, and collectives as *unique*."[23] With the format of the "profile," according to Reckwitz, "the digital subject attempts to demonstrate his or her particular and nonexchangeable personality."[24] The basic thesis of Reckwitz's extensive analysis, according to which late-modern society has in many ways been defined by a logic of the singular and particular, has a number of points of contact with the ideas presented in this book. The troubling development that I have described here – that is, the recent transformation of police and criminological methods of identification into technologies of self-empowerment – can be understood precisely in the sense that Reckwitz has in mind. In today's culture, the social imperative to be "unique" and "authentic" has become so powerful that even certain formats of registration, which had long been reserved for stigmatizing deviant subjects, are now being used to produce this uniqueness – the "profile" as well as the tattoo, location technology as well as devices for measuring bodily functions. Just 50 years ago, all of these methods could have been said to generate individuality only in the sense that they made it possible to recognize deviance. Today they are supposed to guarantee, for each of their users, a fulfilling sense of authentic subjectivity.

In the early 1980s, when Reagan and Thatcher's "new economy" inspired Michel Foucault to formulate his ideas about "governmentality," two concepts were beginning to take hold and merge together. Today they are inextricably linked, and they have done much to redefine our conception of humanity. The first comes from the sphere of the political economy, and the second from the sphere of media technology. The new economic liberalism, which embroiled formerly non-economic sectors of life in the logic of economics, gave rise to increased competition, the rhetoric of self-motivation, and the diminution of the so-called "welfare state." Meanwhile, as Fred Turner has shown, the Californian success story of digital culture hinged on the idea that personal computers and the creation of "virtual communities" were vehicles of personal autonomy and self-empowerment. In the late twentieth century, individuals were thus encouraged from two fronts to emancipate themselves from the constraints of state institutions. This new economic mentality and the vision of cyberspace utopias combined to promote self-government over external government, open competition over government regulation. In the mid-1990s, terminology that had emerged from the political left around 1968 – "self-responsibility," "self-determination," "flat hierarchies" – was adopted by dot-coms and startups and assimilated into the principles of the new economy. Today, this fusion is almost seamless. The free-market economy and the pursuit of profit have formed a proud alliance with the practices of ethics and cultural critique. The figurehead of this collaboration is the "social entrepreneur," a term that itself blends together the social and the economic, and its signature accomplishment is the "sharing economy," which has converted private and seemingly non-monetizable aspects of life – one's own bed, closet, and passenger seat – into lucrative sources of income.[25]

During the Super Bowl on January 22, 1984, Apple introduced its new Macintosh computer in one of the most famous television commercials ever aired. Lasting one minute, the advertisement depicted an Orwellian scene of uniformed party members marching down a hallway full of telescreens to hear an address from "Big Brother." From a gigantic video screen, the latter intones: "Our unification of thoughts is a more powerful weapon than any fleet or army on earth." The camera cuts to a young woman in red running shorts – everything but her is black and white – who is racing toward the screen with a sledge hammer and being chased by the government's henchmen. Just as "Big Brother" is ending his speech, the woman throws the hammer at the screen, causing it to explode. A voiceover makes the following announcement: "On January 24th, Apple Computer will introduce Macintosh. And you'll see why 1984 won't be like *1984*." More than 30 years have passed since then, but from the perspective of today's digital culture it is debatable whether things are really so different from Orwell's prophecy. All around the developed world, people are staring at the same screen in the same casing and are adhering to the same model of self-representation. Having been taken over by individuals, processes of regulation have become more efficient than ever before. The promise of developing our own identities is now a more powerful weapon than the unification of our thoughts.

Notes

All references to online sources were last checked on September 3, 2018.

1 Profiles: The Development of a Format

1 Richard Bélanger et al., "U-Shaped Association Between Intensity of Internet Use and Adolescent Health," *Pediatrics* 127 (2011), 330–5, at 334. For further discussion related to this debate, see the anonymous article "The Mystery of Aurora Suspect's Missing Facebook Account," cnet.com/news/the-mystery-of-aurora-suspects-missing-facebook-account; and Christoph David Piorkowski, "Spurlos im Netz: Wer sich Facebook verweigert, macht sich verdächtig," *Süddeutsche Zeitung* (December 21, 2012), 13.

2 Danah Boyd and Jeffrey Heer, "Profiles as Conversation: Networked Identity Performance on Friendster," in *Proceedings of the 39th Annual Hawaii International Conference on System Sciences* (Los Alamitos: IEEE Computer Society, 2006), n.p. See also Danah Boyd, "Friendster and Publicly Articulated Social Networks," in *CHI 2004 – Connect: Conference Proceedings* (New York: ACM Press, 2004), n.p.; and Danah Boyd and Judith Donath, "Public Displays of Connection," *BT Technology Journal* 22 (2004), 71–82, at 72. These references to Boyd's essays – as well as references to other works relating to the history of the profile – were brought to my attention by Andreas

Weich, whose dissertation on the history of the profile is due to be published shortly. For an overview of some of his findings, see Andreas Weich, "Sich profilieren und profiliert werden: Über zwei Seiten einer Medaille," in *Profile: Interdisziplinäre Beiträge*, ed. Martin Degeling et al. (Lüneburg: Meson Press, 2017), 37–57.

3 Boyd and Donath, "Public Displays of Connection," 74.

4 Boyd and Heer, "Profiles as Conversation," n.p.

5 Eric Partridge and Henry C. Wyld, eds., *Webster Universal Dictionary: Unabridged International Edition* (New York: Harver, 1968), s.v. 'profile' (p. 1163).

6 Rossolimo's study was never translated into English. The quotation here is translated from the German edition: G. I. Rossolimo, *Das psychologische Profil und andere experimentell-psychologische, individuale und kollektive Methoden zur Prüfung der Psychomechanik bei Erwachsenen und Kindern* (Halle an der Saale: C. Marhold, 1926), 8.

7 Karl Bartsch, *Das psychologische Profil und seine Auswertung für Heilpädagogik: Ein Beitrag zur Erforschung der psychischen Funktionen des normalen und abnormalen Kindes*, 2nd edn. (Halle an der Saale: C. Marhold, 1926), 3.

8 The quotations are from ibid., 60, 73; and Fritz Giese, *Psychotechnisches Praktikum* (Halle an der Saale: Wendt & Klauwell, 1923), 40.

9 Louis Gold, "The Psychiatric Profile of the Firesetter," *Journal of Forensic Sciences* 7 (1962), 404–17. On the "mad bomber" and the role that psychoanalysis played in solving the case, see James Brussel, *The Casebook of a Crime Psychiatrist* (New York: Grove Press, 1968).

10 Richard Ault and James Reese, "A Psychological Assessment of Crime: Profiling," *FBI Law Enforcement Bulletin* 49 (1980), 22–5, at 22.

11 Russel Vorpagel, "Painting Psychological Profiles: Charlatanism, Coincidence, Charisma, Chance, or a New Science?" *The Police Chief* 3 (1982), 156–9, at 156.

12 Ault and Reese, "A Psychological Assessment of Crime," 24. For a highly similar list, see Vorpagel, "Painting Psychological Profiles," 159.

13 Gold, "The Psychiatric Profile of the Firesetter," 404, 416.

14 Ault and Reese, "A Psychological Assessment of Crime," 25.

15 Anthony Rider, "The Firesetter: A Psychological Profile," *FBI Law Enforcement Bulletin* 49 (July 1980), 7–17, at 7.

16 On the number of cases in the United States, see Vorpagel, "Painting Psychological Profiles," 159. Regarding the first criminal profile in Germany, see Cornelia Musolff, "Täterprofile

und Fallanalyse: Eine Bestandaufnahme," in *Täterprofile bei Gewaltverbrechen: Mythos, Theorie und Praxis des Profilings*, ed. Cornelia Musolff and Jens Hoffmann (Heidelberg: Springer, 2006), 1–23, at 12.

17 On the history of registering psychiatric patients and on the development of documentary practices in various hospitals during the nineteenth century, see Ali-Reza Ipektschi, "Ärztliche Aufzeichnungen über Patienten im Allgemeinen Krankenhause in Hamburg in der Zeit von 1823–1888" (doctoral diss.: Universität Hamburg, 1983); Brigitte Bernet, "Der Fall des psychiatrischen Formulars," in *Zum Fall machen, zum Fall werden: Wissensproduktion und Patientenerfahrung in Medizin und Psychiatrie des 19. und 20. Jahrhunderts*, ed. Sibylle Brändli et al. (Frankfurt am Main: Campus, 2009), 62–91; Volker Hess, "Formalisierte Beobachtung: Die Genese der modernen Krankenakte am Beispiel der Berliner und Pariser Medizin," *Medizinhistorisches Journal* 45 (2010), 293–340; and Sophie Ledebur, "Schreiben und Beschreiben: Zur epistemischen Funktion von psychiatrischen Krankenakten, ihre Archivierung und deren Übersetzung in Fallgeschichten," *Berichte zur Wissenschaftsgeschichte* 34 (2011), 102–24.

18 J. C. Lavater, *Von der Physiognomik* (Leipzig: Weidmann, 1772), 63. This early work on physiognomy, which has not been translated into English, is distinct from Lavater's more comprehensive treatment of the subject, which appeared in multiple English editions under the title *Essays on Physiognomy*.

19 Alphonse Bertillon, *La photographie judiciare avec un appendice sur la classification et l'identification anthropométrique* (Paris: Gauthier-Villars, 1890), 17.

20 Here one could add yet a third level of meaning to the concept, which concerns the grooved or "profile" bicycle tires first patented by Dunlop or Palmer in 1880. In the Sherlock Holmes story "The Adventure of the Priory School," it is the interpretation of these peculiar treads near the crime scene that sets the detective on the right track toward finding the missing pupil. At one point in the investigation, Holmes remarks: "I am familiar with forty-two different impressions left by tyres." Quoted from Arthur Conan Doyle, "The Adventure of the Priory School," in *The Return of Sherlock Holmes* (New York: A. Wessels, 1907), 119–58, at 136.

21 For a screenshot of Match.com's homepage from 1995, see Mia de Graaf, "'I Was Trying to Find the Right Person to Marry': Match.com Co-Founder Reveals the Inspiration of Online Dating Site as It Goes Public," *Daily Mail* (November 19, 2015): www.dailymail.co.uk/sciencetech/article-3324447/

l-trying-right-person-marry-Match-com-founder-reveals-inspiration-online-dating-site-goes-public.html. The quotation of the 1996 advertisement was taken from a web page that is no longer active: kremen.com/wp-content/uploads/fi les/019_WEBSIGHT_0996_MATCH_AD.PDF. For a report about using the site, see Leslie Crawford, "Geek Love," *San Francisco Focus* (October, 1996), 20: "You simply post your profile on-line and wait for the on-line love letters."

22 See Eva Illouz, *Cold Intimacies: The Making of Emotional Capitalism* (Cambridge: Polity, 2007), 74–114; and Illouz, *Why Love Hurts: A Sociological Explanation* (Cambridge: Polity, 2012), 198–237.

23 See youtube.com/watch?v=MzE2cOqUFWM, at the 2:20 mark.

24 Older online communities such as WELL ("Whole Earth 'Lectronic Link"), which was founded in California in 1985, did not make use of the profile format. Members dialed in with a user name and password and could comb through various thematically arranged sites and post comments. See Howard Rheingold, *The Virtual Community: Homesteading on the Electronic Frontier*, 2nd edn. (Cambridge, MA: MIT Press, 2000), 1–24; and Fred Turner, *From Counterculture to Cyberculture: Steward Brand, the Whole Earth Network, and the Rise of Digital Utopianism* (University of Chicago Press, 2008), 141–74.

25 Andrew Weinreich, "Method and Apparatus for Constructing a Networking Database and System," United States Patent No. US6175831 (1997). The patent can be read online at www.google.com/patents/US6175831.

26 See Teresa Riordan, "Idea for Online Networking Brings Two Entrepreneurs Together," *New York Times* (December 1, 2003): www.nytimes.com/2003/12/01/technology/technology-media-patents-idea-for-online-networking-brings-two-entrepreneurs.html. Reid Hoffmann, who is still the president of LinkedIn, has remained the owner of this patent ever since.

27 Weinreich, "Method and Apparatus for Constructing a Networking Database and System," n.p.

28 The idea first appeared in a short story titled "Chain-Links" by the Hungarian author Frigyes Karinthy.

29 These works have not been translated into English. Their original German titles are, respectively, *Souverän im Vorstellungsgespräch*, *Erfolgreich im Assessment-Center*, and *Das große Bewerbungshandbuch*.

30 Christian Püttjer and Uwe Schnierda, *Anschreiben und Lebensläufe für Hochschulabsolventen* (Felde am Westensee: Sit-Up Verlag, 1999).

31 Among others, the following books have appeared in various editions: *Die Bewerbungsmappe mit Profil für Führungskräfte* ["The Job-Application Portfolio with a Profile for Executives"], *Die Bewerbungsmappe mit Profil für Hochschulabsolventen (mit Insiderkommentaren)* ["The Job-Application Portfolio with a Profile for College Graduates (with Insider Commentary)"], *Das große Bewerbungshandbuch (mit Püttjer & Schnierda-Profil-Methode)* ["The Definitive Job-Application Handbook (with the Püttjer & Schnierda Profile Method)"], *20 perfekte Bewerbungen mit Profil* ["Twenty Perfect Job Applications with a Profile"], *Die Bewerbungsmappe mit Profil für Um- und Aufsteiger* ["The Job-Application Portfolio with a Profile for Those Seeking to Transfer Jobs or Earn a Promotion"], *Vorstellungsgespräch: Vorbereiten, überzeugen, gewinnen (mit Pütter & Schnierda-Profil-Methode)* ["Interviews: Prepare, Persuade, Succeed (with the Püttjer & Schnierda Profile Method)"].

32 Püttjer provided me with this information in a telephone interview conducted on January 26, 2017.

33 Christian Püttjer and Uwe Schnierda, *Das große Bewerbungshandbuch*, 2nd edn. (Frankfurt am Main: Campus, 2006), 25.

34 Christian Püttjer and Uwe Schnierda, *Das gelungene Online-Bewerbung* (Frankfurt am Main: Campus, 2001), 85; Püttjer and Schnierda, *Das große Bewerbungshandbuch*, 20.

35 Püttjer and Schnierda, *Das große Bewerbungshandbuch*, 25.

36 See, for example, Püttjer and Schnierda, *Anschreiben und Lebensläufe für Hochschulabsolventen*, 79; and Püttjer and Schnierda, *Das große Bewerbungshandbuch*, 18, 220.

37 The term "user profile," for instance, can be found in demographic analyses as early as the 1970s. See Janpeter Kob et al., *Profil der Benutzer öffentlicher Bibliotheken* (Berlin: Deutscher Bibliotheksverband, 1973).

38 See, for instance, John Burnett and Alan Bush, "Profiling the Yuppies," *Journal of Advertising Research* 26 (1986), 27–35.

39 Andreas Wenzlau et al., *KundenProfiling: Die Methode zur Neukundenakquise* (Erlangen: Publicis, 2003), 17–18 (emphasis original).

40 See "Using Information from User Video Game Interactions to Target Advertisements," United States Patent No. WO 2007041371 A3 (2007). Regarding the implications of this method, see Helmut Martin-Jung, "Verhaltensforschung," *Süddeutsche Zeitung* (May 15, 2007), 1. The patent can be viewed online at https://www.google.com/patents/WO2007041371A3?cl=en.

41 Petra Wittig, "Die datenschutzrechtliche Problematik der Anfertigung von Persönlichkeitsprofilen," *Recht der Datenverarbeitung* 16 (2000), 61–9, at 62. In this passage, Wittig is in part citing the opinion of another lawyer.

42 Christoph Schnabel, *Datenschutz bei profilbasierten Location Based Services: Die datenschutzadäquate Gestaltung von Service-Plattformen für Mobilkommunikation* (Kassel University Press, 2009), 172, 171.

43 "Regulation (EU) 2016/679 of the European Parliament and of the Council of 27 April 2016 on the Protection of Natural Persons with Regard to the Processing of Personal Data and on the Free Movement of Such Data, and Repealing Directive 95/46/EC (General Data Protection Regulation)" (2016): http://eur-lex.europa.eu/legal-content/EN/TXT/?uri=CELEX:32016R0679, §71, §60, respectively.

44 Ibid., §18.

45 Schnabel, *Datenschutz bei profilbasierten Location Based Services*, 177. In terms of privacy law, one of the first studies to discuss the coexistence of unwittingly and actively created profiles is Louis Specht, *Konsequenzen der Ökonomisierung informationeller Selbstbestimmung: Die zivilrechtliche Erfassung des Datenhandels* (Cologne: Heymann, 2012).

46 Michal Kosinski et al., "Our Twitter Profiles, Ourselves: Predicting Personality with Twitter," in *IEEE Third International Conference on Social Computing* (Los Alamitos: IEEE Computer Society, 2011), 180–5.

47 Michal Kosinski et al., "Private Traits and Attributes Are Predictable from Digital Records of Human Behavior," *Proceedings of the National Academy of Sciences* 111 (2013), 5802–5, at 5802. See also the project's website at http://mypersonality.org/wiki/doku.php.

48 Kosinski et al., "Private Traits and Attributes," 5802.

49 Kosinski et al., "Our Twitter Profiles," 185 (emphasis original).

50 Quoted from Alexander Nix, "The Power of Big Data and Psychographics in the Electoral Process," a presentation delivered at the 2016 Concordia Summit. The presentation can be viewed on YouTube at https://www.youtube.com/watch?v=n8Dd5aVXLCc, and the citation here is taken from the 4:04 mark. For a discussion of Cambridge Analytica's methods, see Hannes Grassegger and Mikael Krogerus, "Ich habe nur gezeigt, dass es die Bombe gibt," *Das Magazin* 48/3 (December 3, 2016): https://www.dasmagazin.ch/2016/12/03/ich-habe-nur-gezeigt-dass-es-die-bombe-gibt.

51 Sherry Turkle, *Life on the Screen: Identity in the Age of the Internet* (New York: Simon & Schuster, 1995), 185.

52 Ibid.

53 Sherry Turkle, "Constructions and Reconstructions of Self in Virtual Reality: Playing in the MUDS," *Mind, Culture, and Activity* 1 (1994), 158–67, at 164 (emphasis original).
54 Rheingold, *The Virtual Community*, 149.
55 John Perry Barlow, "A Declaration of the Independence of Cyberspace," Electronic Frontier Foundation (February 8, 1996): https://www.eff.org/cyberspace-independence.
56 Turner, *From Counterculture to Cyberculture*, 162.
57 Ibid., 117.
58 Barlow, "A Declaration of the Independence of Cyberspace," n.p.
59 Quoted from https://www.facebook.com/legal/terms.
60 David Kirkpatrick, *The Facebook Effect: The Inside Story of the Company that Is Connecting the World* (New York: Simon & Schuster, 2010), 100.
61 Ibid., 199.
62 Ibid., 210.

2 Locations: GPS and the Aesthetics of Suspicion

1 Quoted from https://support.apple.com/en-ca/HT207056.
2 F. Sender, "Von TRANSIT zu NAVSTAR: Entwicklungstendenzen der Satellitennavigation," *Ortung und Navigation* 2 (1978), 318–38, at 318.
3 See Krüger, "Zweckmäßiger Einsatz und Betrieb von Radaranlagen," *Ortung und Navigation* 2 (1978), 105–20, at 105.
4 Friedrich Kittler, *Gramophone, Film, Typewriter*, trans. Geoffrey Winthrop-Young and Michael Wutz (Stanford University Press, 1999), 97.
5 H. C. Freiesleben, "Das Satelliten-System NAVSTAR/GPS," *Ortung und Navigation* 2 (1978), 63–79, at 66; D. Ernst, "NAVSTAR/GPS (Global Positioning System) und elektronische Störmaßnahmen," *Ortung und Navigation* 2 (1978), 409–26, at 409; and Jan Peter Tjardts, "NAVSTAR GPS: Entwicklungsstand und weitere Zukunft dieses globalen Navigationssystems," *Ortung und Navigation* 6 (1982), 148–58, at 150, respectively.
6 A representative publication in this regard, and the source of the quotation above about Ronald Reagan, is John Beukers, "The Unfolding Future of the Global Navigation Satellite System – Part I: From the Past to the Present," *GPS Solutions* 1 (1995), 23–7, at 25.

7 *Presidential Decision Directive NSTC-6* (March 28, 1996), fas.org/spp/military/docops/national/gps.htm.

8 The White House, Official Press Secretary, Press Briefing (May 1, 2000), www.presidency.ucsb.edu/ws/?pid=48120.

9 *Public Urban Locator Service (PULSE): Background and Conference Proceedings* (New York: The Institute of Public Administration, 1968), 28; quoted from Ralph K. Schwitzgebel, *Development and Legal Regulation of Coercive Behavior Modification Techniques with Offenders* (Rockville, MD: National Institute of Mental Health, 1971), 18.

10 G. R. Hansen and W. G. Leflang, *Application of Automatic Vehicle Location in Law Enforcement: An Introductory Planning Guide* (Washington, DC: United States Department of Justice, 1976), 4.

11 Bernd Eylert, "Standortbestimmung von Einsatzfahrzeugen," *Die Polizei* 73 (1982), B13–B19, at B13. See also Hansen and Leflang, *Application of Automatic Vehicle Location*, 1 (here the authors note that "officer safety" is one of the system's "primary features"); and W. Fogy, "Positionsbestimmung von Einsatzfahrzeugen im urbanen Gelände," *Ortung und Navigation* 2 (1978), 500–19, which seems to be the first German essay devoted to the topic.

12 Konrad Peitz, "Bedeutung moderner Ortungs- und Nativigationstechnologien für Gewährleistung der öffentlichen Sicherheit und Ordnung," *Die Polizei* 78 (1987), 361–3, at 361.

13 For a discussion of these cases, see John Hall, "Electronic Tracking Devices: Following the Fourth Amendment," *FBI Law Enforcement Journal* 54/2 (1985), 26–31.

14 John W. Lavrakis and Glenn C. Marshall, "Where Is It and Where Is It Going? A Comprehensive Look at GPS Asset Location," *GPS Solutions* 1 (1995), 121–8, at 122.

15 Ibid.

16 Ibid.

17 Ibid., 124.

18 See Paul Larkin, "The Fourth Amendment and New Technology," *Legal Memorandum* 102 (2013), 1–9, at 3.

19 Quoted from Hall, "Electronic Tracking Devices," 27.

20 Ibid.

21 *United States* v. *Jones*, 565 U.S. ___, No. 10-1259 (2012), 10 (Court Opinion).

22 Ibid., 10 (Alito's Concurrence).

23 Ibid.

24 Ibid., 11.

25 Ibid., 12.

26 *United States* v. *Jones* (transcript of arguments heard on November 8, 2011), 44.

27 *United States* v. *Jones* (Alito's Concurrence), 13.
28 *United States* v. *Jones* (Sotomayor's Concurrence), 3.
29 See Carrie Johnson, "FBI Still Struggling with Supreme Court's GPS Ruling," National Public Radio (March 21, 2012): www.npr.org/2012/03/21/149011887/fbi-still-struggling-with-supreme-courts-gps-ruling.
30 *Criminal Procedure Code (Strafprozeßordnung, StPO)*, official translation by the Federal Ministry of Justice (of the version published on April 7, 1987 with amendments incorporated up to September 7, 1998), §100c. The text is available online.
31 *Bundesverfassungsbericht* 2 BvR 581/01 (2005).
32 See the following press release: "Bundesgerichtshof: Überwachung von Personen mittels an Fahrzeugen angebrachter GPS-Empfänger ist grundsätzlich strafbar," *Bundesgerichtshof: Mitteilung der Pressestelle* 96 (2013): http://juris.bundesgerichtshof.de/cgi-bin/rechtsprechung/document.py?Gericht=bgh&Art=pm&Datum=2013&Sort=3&nr=64248&pos=0&anz=95.
33 Ralph K. Schwitzgebel et al., "A Program of Research in Behavioral Electronics," *Behavioral Science* 9 (1964), 233–8, at 233.
34 Ralph K. Schwitzgebel and William Hurd, "Behavioral Supervision System with Wrist Carried Transceiver," U.S. Patent No. 3478344A (1969). The patent can be read online at www.google.ch/patents/US3478344.
35 Ralph K. Schwitzgebel, "Development of an Electronic Rehabilitation System for Parolees," *Law and Computer Technology* 2/3 (1969), 9–12, at 10.
36 Schwitzgebel, *Development and Legal Regulation of Coercive Behavior Modification Techniques*.
37 Schwitzgebel, "Development of an Electronic Rehabilitation System," 12.
38 Schwitzgebel et al., "A Program of Research in Behavioral Electronics," 237.
39 See Rich Johnston, "When Spider-Man Invented Electronic Tagging," *Bleeding Cool* (June 24, 2012): https://www.bleedingcool.com/2012/06/24/when-spider-man-invented-electronic-tagging. On Jack Love and his inspiration from *Spider-Man*, see also Francis Timko, "Electronic Monitoring – How It All Began: Conversations with Love and Gross," *Journal of Probation and Parole* 17 (1985), 15–16; and Richard Fox, "Dr. Schwitzgebel's Machine Revisited: Electronic Monitoring of Offenders," *Australian and New Zealand Journal of Criminology* 20 (1987), 131–47.
40 Annette Jolin and Robert Rogers, "Elektronisch überwachter Hausarrest: Darstellung einer Strafvollzugsalternative in den Vereinigten Staaten," *Monatsschrift für Kriminologie und Strafrechtreform* 73 (1990), 201–9, at 202.

41 According to Fox, "Dr. Schwitzgebel's Machine Revisited," 133, the bracelets at the time weighed around 100 grams.
42 *Bundestagsdrucksache* 17/3403 (2010).
43 Achim Brauneisen, "Die elektronische Überwachung des Aufenthaltsortes als neues Instrument der Führungsaufsicht," *Strafverteidiger* 31 (2011), 311–16, at 311.
44 *German Criminal Code*, trans. Michael Bohlander (the version is that published on November 13, 1988, with amendments incorporated up to October 10, 2013), §68b. The text is available online at https://www.gesetze-im-internet.de/englisch_stgb/englisch_stgb.html#p0541.
45 Detlef Nogala and Rita Haverkamp, "Elektronische Bewachung: Stichworte zur punitiven Aufenthaltskontrolle von Personen," *Datenschutz und Datensicherheit* 24 (2000), 31–8, at 35.
46 Brauneisen, "Die elektronische Überwachung," 312. For a nearly identical comparison to a wristwatch, see Torsten Kunze, "Die electronische Fußfessel in Hessen: Eine positive Betrachtung über Haftvermeidung mit Hilfe zur Selbsthilfe," *Forum Strafvollzug* 57 (2008), 33–5, at 34.
47 See Günes Önel, "Verfassungsmäßigkeit und Effektivität der 'elektronischen Fußfessel,'" *Jahrbuch des kriminalwissenschaftlichen Institut der Leibniz Universität Hannover* (2012): http://edok01.tib.uni-hannover.de/edoks/e01dh13/76776479Xl.pdf. This is also the reason why no one has yet filed a lawsuit against the use of "electronic ankle bracelets," something that cannot be said about the surreptitious surveillance of suspects.
48 Brauneisen, "Die elektronische Überwachung," 312.
49 Quoted from ibid., 313.
50 Thomas Feltes, "Kriminalität und soziale Kontrolle im 21. Jahrhundert: Eine futuristisches Szenario vor dem Hintergrund aktueller Entwicklungen," *Bewährungshilfe* 35 (1988), 90–102, at 90, 95, 97, respectively.
51 These topics are discussed in greater detail in the fourth chapter of this book.
52 Feltes, "Kriminalität und soziale Kontrolle," 102.
53 Len Jacobson, "GPS: The World's New Utility," *GPS Solutions* 1 (1995), 81.
54 Regine Buschauer and Katharine Willis, *Locative Media: Medialität und Räumlichkeit – Multidisziplinäre Perspectiven zur Verortung der Medien* (Bielefeld: Transcript, 2013), 7. See also Regine Buschauer, "(Very) Nervous Systems: Big Mobile Data," in *Big Data: Analysen zum digitalen Wandel von Wissen, Macht und Ökonomie*, ed. Rámon Reichert (Bielefeld: Transcript, 2014), 405–36, in which the author outlines the prehistory of using cell phones as tracking devices. Well into the 1990s, one

of the purely infrastructural problems of cellular technology was that one phone had to know the location of the other – otherwise, of course, the system would not be able to function. It was not until the second half of the 1990s, according to Buschauer, that location methods began to be used as an end in themselves and came to be perceived as one of the "core capabilities" of digital culture.

55 Jordan Frith, *Smartphones as Locative Media* (Cambridge: Polity, 2015), 29. See also Diep Dao et al., "Location-Based Services: Technical and Business Issues," *GPS Solutions* 6 (2002), 169–78, at 169; and Gerard Lachapelle and Jinling Wang, "Letter from the Guest Editors: The GPS Wireless Special Issue," *GPS Solutions* 6 (2002), 137.

56 Frith, *Smartphones as Locative Media*, 34.

57 Nicholas Negroponte, *Being Digital* (New York: Knopf, 1995), 6–7.

58 See, for instance, Judith Ackermann, "Location-Based Mobile Gaming in der Stadt: Spielerische Eroberung des urbanen Raums und Hybrid Reality Theatre," in *Mobile Medien – Mobiles Leben: Neue Technologien, Mobilität und die mediatisierte Gesellschaft*, ed. Thomas Christian Bächle and Caja Thimm (Munster: LIT Verlag, 2014), 143–67, at 156.

59 For a popular guide to playing the game, see Kristian Köhntopp et al., "Ingress – Die Kunst, Umwege zu gehen" (June 22, 2015): http://youarethekey.de/wp-content/uploads/2015/09/Ingress-dieKunstUmwegezugehen.pdf.

60 Luc Boltanski, *Mysteries and Conspiracies: Detective Stories, Spy Novels, and the Making of Modern Societies*, trans. Catherine Porter (Cambridge: Polity, 2014), 23. Regarding the evidential paradigm, see Carlo Ginzburg, "Clues: Roots of an Evidential Paradigm," in *Clues, Myths, and the Historical Method*, trans. John Tedeschi and Anne C. Tedeschi (Baltimore: Johns Hopkins University Press, 1989), 87–113.

61 Detlef Nogala and Fritz Sack, "Folgerungen für die polizeiliche Arbeit aus der Technikausstattung," in *Aktuelle Methoden der Kriminaltechnik und Kriminalistik*, ed. Heinrich Schielke (Wiesbaden: Bundeskriminalamt, 1995), 115–68, at 127, 149.

3 Cavity Searches: Bodily Measurements and the Quantified-Self Movement

1 Gary Wolf, "The Data-Driven Life," *The New York Times Magazine* (April 28, 2010): www.nytimes.com/2010/05/02/magazine/02self-measurement-t.html.

2 Georg Christoph Lichtenberg, "Über Physiognomik – Wider die Physiognomen: Zu Beförderung der Menschenliebe und Menschenkenntnis," in *Schriften und Briefe*, vol. III, ed. Wolfgang Promies (Munich: Hanser, 1972; orig. published in 1778), 256–95, at 288.
3 Wolf, "The Data-Driven Life," n.p.
4 For these figures, see Gina Neff and Dawn Nafus, *Self-Tracking* (Cambridge, MA: MIT Press, 2016), 1; Gary Marshall, "The Story of Fitbit: How a Wooden Box Became a $4 Billion Company," *Wearable: Tech for Your Connected Self* (September 9, 2016): https://www.wearable.com/fitbit/youre-fitbit-and-you-know-it-how-a-wooden-box-became-a-dollar-4-billion-company; and Anonymous, "Number of Fitbit Devices Sold Worldwide from 2010 to 2017": https://www.statista.com/statistics/472591/fitbit-devices-sold.
5 Wolf, "The Data-Driven Life," n.p.
6 Quoted from https://www.fitbit.com/en-ca/whyfitbit.
7 Quoted from https://www.youtube.com/watch?v=K0qVi_nF6y8.
8 Quoted from https://www.fitbit.com/en-ca/whyfitbit.
9 On the history of the scale, see Hillel Schwartz, *Never Satisfied: A Cultural History of Diets, Fantasies, and Fat* (New York: Free Press, 1986), 164–77. For a comparison between previous and current methods of self-tracking, see Kate Crawford et al., "Our Metrics, Ourselves: A Hundred Years of Self-Tracking from the Weight Scale to the Wrist Wearable Device," *European Journal of Cultural Studies* 18 (2015), 479–96.
10 This quotation, which was taken in 2017 from the German version of Fitbit's webpage (https://www.fitbit.com/de/app), is no longer on the site.
11 Quoted from https://www.fitbit.com/en-ca/app.
12 Ibid.
13 Quoted from https://www.fitbit.com/en-ca/whyfitbit.
14 Richard MacManus, *Health Trackers: How Technology Is Helping Us Monitor and Improve Our Health* (London: Rowman and Littlefield, 2014), 13.
15 See https://generalivitality.com.
16 Quoted from https://www.generali.de/ueber-generali/presse-medien/pressemitteilungen/versicherung-neu-denken—generali-vitality-geht-an-den-start-10844.
17 See Mirko Wenig, "TK will Verwendung von Fitnesstrackern im Bonusprogramm belohnen," *Versicherungsbote: Information für Versicherungsmakler* (August 24, 2016): https://www.versicherungsbote.de/id/4844671/Techniker-Krankenkasse-Fitnesstracker-Bonusprogramm.
18 Regarding Dacadoo's "health score," see the company's website at https://www.dacadoo.com.

19 See Ulrich Bröckling, "Prävention," in *Glossar der Gegenwart*, ed. Susanne Krasmann et al. (Frankfurt am Main: Suhrkamp, 2004), 7–40; Bröckling, *Das unternehmerische Selbst: Soziologie einer Subjektivierungsform* (Frankfurt am Main: Suhrkamp, 2007); and Thomas Lemke, "Test," in *Glossar der Gegenwart*, ed. Krasmann et al., 263–70.

20 Quoted from https://generalivitality.de/vmp/bewusst_machen/vitality_alter.

21 Neff and Nafus, *Self-Tracking*, 15.

22 Quoted from https://www.youtube.com/watch?v=YN_MjyNq3Z8 (beginning at the 3:10 mark).

23 Hugo Münsterberg, *On the Witness Stand: Essays on Psychology and Crime* (New York: Clark Boardman, 1923), 6.

24 Ibid., 3.

25 Hugo Münsterberg, *Grundzüge der Psychotechnik*, 2nd edn. (Leipzig: J. A. Barth, 1920), 236.

26 Hans Kurella, *Cesare Lombroso und die Naturgeschichte des Verbrechers* (Hamburg: J. F. Richter, 1892), 11.

27 Stephen Jay Gould, *The Mismeasure of Man*, 2nd edn. (New York: W. W. Norton, 1996), 153.

28 For a list of these types, see Kurella, *Cesare Lombroso und die Naturgeschichte des Verbrechers*, 39.

29 Alphonse Bertillon, *Das anthropometrische Signalement: Neue Methode zu Identitäts-Feststellungen. Vortrag am internationalen Congresse für Straf- und Gefängniswesen zu Rom abgehalten* (Berlin: Fischer, 1890), 4.

30 Ibid., 11.

31 Ibid., 4–5.

32 Manfred Schneider, *Die erkaltete Herzensschrift: Der autobiographische Text im 20. Jahrhundert* (Munich: C. Hanser, 1986), 23.

33 Bertillon, *Das anthropometrische Signalement*, 30–1.

34 Marcel Krause, "Einleitung Sektion 5: Messen," in *Menschenversuche: Eine Anthologie, 1750–2000*, ed. Nicolas Pethes et al. (Frankfurt am Main: Suhrkamp, 2008), 355–90, at 362.

35 Hans Gross, *Criminal Investigation: A Practical Handbook*, trans. John Adam and J. Collyer Adam (Madras: A. Krishnamachari, 1906), 37.

36 Ibid., 24.

37 Ibid.

38 Ibid., 144 (emphasis original).

39 Ibid.

40 Richard Krafft-Ebing, *Beiträge zur Erkennung und richtigen forensischen Beurtheilung krankhafter Gemütszustände für Aerzte, Richter und Vertheidiger* (Erlangen: Enke, 1867), 19.

41 Carl Westphal, "Eigenthümliche mit Einschlafen verbundene Einfälle," in *Carl Westphal's gesammelte Abhandlungen*, ed. Alexander Westphal (Berlin: Hirschwald, 1892; orig. published in 1877), 393–407, at 393.
42 Ibid., 394. On the significance of obsessive counting in early-twentieth-century psychiatry, see Walter Jahrreiß, "Über Zwangsvorstellungen im Verlauf der Schizophrenie," *Archiv für Psychiatrie und Nervenkrankheiten* 77 (1936), 740–88.
43 Georg Joachim, *Über Zwangsvorstellungen* (Berlin: Schade, 1892), 25–6.
44 Jahrreiß, "Über Zwangsvorstellungen im Verlauf der Schizophrenie," 761.
45 Ibid., 782.
46 Ibid., 783.
47 Alfred Döblin, "The Murder of a Buttercup," trans. Patrick O'Neill, in *Early 20th Century German Fiction*, ed. Alexander Stephan (New York: Continuum, 2003), 57–67, at 57.
48 Reiner Marx, "Literatur und Zwangsneurose: Eine Gegenübertragungs-Improvisation zu Alfred Döblins früher Erzählung 'Die Ermordung einer Butterblume,'" in *Internationales Alfred-Döblin-Kolloquium, Leiden 1995*, ed. Gabrielle Sander (Bern: Peter Lang, 1997), 49–60, at 55. Here Marx is referring in particular to John Duytschaever, "Eine Pionierleistung des Expressionismus: Alfred Döblins Erzählung 'Die Ermordung einer Butterblume,'" *Amsterdamer Beiträge zur neueren Germanistik* 2 (1973), 27–43.
49 Döblin, "The Murder of a Buttercup," 58. Incidentally, Michael Fischer is not the only unstable protagonist in Döblin's work who compulsively counts his steps. In his long historical novel *November 18*, for instance, the following remark is made about the protagonist Friedrich Becker: "As he was counting and controlling his steps, he quickly turned around to see what was happening behind his back." Quoted from Wolfgang Schäffner, *Die Ordnung des Wahns: Zur Poetologie psychiatrischen Wissens bei Alfred Döblin* (Munich: Fink, 1995), 44.
50 The patient is quoted in Wilhelm Griesinger, "Über einen wenig bekannten psychopathischen Zustand," *Archiv für Psychiatrie und Nervenkrankheiten* 1 (1868), 626–35, at 631.
51 Westphal, "Eigenthümliche mit Einschlafen verbundene Einfälle," 405.
52 Sigmund Freud, "The Neuro-Psychoses of Defence," in *The Standard Edition of the Complete Psychological Works of Sigmund Freud, Volume III (1893–1899): Early Psycho-Analytic Publications*, ed. James Strachey (London: The Hogarth Press, 1962), 41–61, at 47.

53 Sigmund Freud, "Further Remarks on the Neuro-Psychoses of Defence," in *The Standard Edition of the Complete Psychological Works of Sigmund Freud, Volume III (1893–1899): Early Psycho-Analytic Publications*, ed. James Strachey (London: The Hogarth Press, 1962), 157–85, at 169.
54 Alexandre Cullerre, "Les épileptiques arithmomanes," *Annales médico-psychologiques: Septième série* 11 (1890), 25–36; quoted here from Julius Donath, "Über Arithmomanie," *Zeitschrift für die gesamte Neurologie und Psychiatrie* 43 (1918), 56–64, at 56.
55 Leopold Löwenfeld, *Die psychischen Zwangserscheinungen* (Wiesbaden: J. F. Bergmann, 1904), 230–1.
56 Freud, "Further Remarks on the Neuro-Psychoses of Defence," 173.
57 Gould, *The Mismeasure of Man*, 139.
58 Ibid., 27, 56.
59 Ibid., 300.
60 Ibid., 106.
61 Ibid.
62 Ibid., 183.
63 Ibid., 189.
64 Ibid., 213.
65 Wolf, "The Data-Driven Life," n.p.
66 Münsterberg, *Grundzüge der Psychotechnik*, 236. See also the similar passages in ibid., 507; and Münsterberg, *On the Witness Stand*, 81–2.
67 John B. Watson, "Psychology as the Behaviorist Views It," *Psychological Review* 20 (1913), 158–77, at 163.
68 John B. Watson, *Behaviorism* (New York: Norton, 1925), 5.
69 Watson, "Psychology as the Behaviorist Views It," 158.
70 B. F. Skinner, *About Behaviorism* (New York: Vintage Books, 1974), 16.
71 Ulrich Raulff, "Münsterbergs Erfindung oder Der elektrifizierte Zeuge," *Freibeuter* 24 (1985), 33–42, at 39.
72 Skinner, *About Behaviorism*, 185.
73 Ibid., 248.
74 Quoted from the following press release: "Generali, European Partner with Discovery" (November 18, 2014): https://www.generali.com/media/press-releases/all/2014/Generali-European-partnership-with-Discovery.
75 Münsterberg, *Grundzüge der Psychotechnik*, 216.
76 Watson, *Behaviorism*, 10–11.
77 Skinner, *About Behaviorism*, 247.
78 Quoted from https://www.fitbit.com/en-ca/app.

79 See Thomas Penzel, "Schlafforschung heute: Entwicklungen, Techniken und Motivationen der Praxis," in *Kontrollgewinn – Kontrollverlust: Die Geschichte des Schlafs in der Moderne*, ed. Hannah Ahlheim (Frankfurt am Main: Campus, 2014), 209–26, at 213. The manual in question is Allen Rechtschaffen and Anthony Kales, eds., *A Manual of Standardized Terminology, Techniques, and Scoring System for Sleep Stages of Human Subjects* (Bethesda: US Department of Health, Education, and Welfare, 1968).
80 Quoted from http://sleep.urbandroid.org/documentation/core/sleep-tracking.
81 Wolf, "The Data-Driven Life," n.p.
82 Münsterberg, *Grundzüge der Psychotechnik*, 237.
83 Münsterberg, *On the Witness Stand*, 45–6.
84 See Raulff, "Münsterbergs Erfindung," 36.
85 Münsterberg, *Grundzüge der Psychotechnik*, 506–7.
86 Ibid., 502.
87 Ibid.
88 Quoted from Raulff, "Münsterbergs Erfindung," 33.
89 Ibid., 42.
90 Kate Crawford, "When Fitbit Is the Expert Witness," *The Atlantic* (November 19, 2014): https://www.theatlantic.com/technology/archive/2014/11/when-fitbit-is-the-expert-witness/382936.
91 For this point of view, see Parmy Olson, "Fitbit Now Being Used in the Courtroom," *Forbes* (November 16, 2014): https://www.forbes.com/sites/parmyolson/2014/11/16/fitbit-data-court-room-personal-injury-claim/#1a91f3d27379.
92 Crawford, "When Fitbit Is the Expert Witness," n.p.
93 Jacob Siegal, "One Woman's Fitbit Just Decided a Criminal Case," *BGR* (April 20, 2016): http://bgr.com/2016/04/20/fitbit-fitness-tracker-legal-case.
94 Kashmir Hill, "Fitbit Data Just Undermined a Woman's Rape Claim," *Splinter* (June 29, 2015): https://splinternews.com/fitbit-data-just-undermined-a-womans-rape-claim-1793848735.

4 The Forgotten Fear of Registration

1 Anonymous, "Datenschrott für eine Milliarde?" *Der Spiegel* 12 (1987), 30–53, at 30.
2 Verena Rottmann and Holger Strohm, *Was Sie gegen Mikrozensus und Volkszählung tun können* (Frankfurt am Main: Zweitausendeins, 1987), 7.
3 Ibid., 136.

4 Ibid., 9.
5 Ibid., 11–12.
6 Franz Koppenstedt, "Keine unzumutbaren Fragen bei der Volkszählung," *Frankfurter Allgemeine Zeitung* (April 12, 1983), 7.
7 This ruling by the Federal Constitutional Court, which was issued on December 15, 1983, can be read online at https://openjur.de/u/268440.html.
8 Images of the forms can be viewed at https://www.deutsche-digitale-bibliothek.de/item/UBKXLYCVA5QTY4B7CX2FWXLXBM7OOCLD. All of the quotations here have been taken from this website.
9 Anonymous, "Datenschrott für eine Milliarde?" 31. On the events in Leverkusen, see ibid., 30. On the events in Freiburg, see the report in *Dossier Volkszählung '87* (Duisburg: Universität Duisburg Gesamtschule, 1988), n.p.
10 Weinreich, "Method and Apparatus for Constructing a Networking Database and System."
11 Rottmann and Strohm, *Was Sie gegen Mikrozensus und Volkszählung tun können*, 7.
12 Anonymous, "Datenschrott für eine Milliarde?" 53.
13 Rottmann and Strohm, *Was Sie gegen Mikrozensus und Volkszählung tun können*, 126.
14 Claus Fokke Wermann, "Schöne neue Kabelwelt," in *Volkszählungs-Boykott: Bilder, Plakate, Flugschriten* (Kassel: n.p., 1987), 37–9, at 38.
15 Rottmann and Strohm, *Was Sie gegen Mikrozensus und Volkszählung tun können*, 9.
16 Götz Aly and Karl Heinz Roth, *The Nazi Census: Identification and Control in the Third Reich*, trans. Assenka Oksiloff (Philadelphia: Temple University Press, 2004), 6. Originally published as *Die restlose Erfassung: Volkszählen, Identifizieren, Aussondern im Nationalsozialismus* (Berlin: S. Fischer, 1984).
17 Aly and Roth, *The Nazi Census*, 7.
18 Ibid., 56.
19 Götz Aly, "Die restlose Erfassung im Nationalsozialismus," in *Volkszählungs-Boykott: Bilder, Plakate, Flugschriten* (Kassel: n.p., 1987), 12–16.
20 Rottmann and Strohm, *Was Sie gegen Mikrozensus und Volkszählung tun können*, 8.
21 Horst Herold, "Organisatorische Grundzüge der elektronischen Datenverarbeitung im Bereich der Polizei: Versuch eines Zukunftsmodells," *Taschenbuch für Kriminalisten* 18 (1968), 240–54, at 244–5.
22 Ibid., 243.
23 Ibid., 240.

24 Horst Herold, "'Rasterfahndung' – Eine computergestützte Fahndungsform der Polizei," *Recht und Politik* 21 (1985), 84–97, at 85.
25 Anonymous, "Datenschrott für eine Milliarde?" 53.
26 Freimut Duve, "Katalysator gegen den Orwell-Staat," in *Die Volkszählung*, ed. Jürgen Taeger (Reinbek bei Hamburg: Rowohlt, 1983), 25–30, at 26.
27 Eva Hubert, "Politiker fragen – Bürger antworten nicht! Die Boycottbewegung gegen die Volkszählung," in *Die Volkszählung*, ed. Jürgen Taeger (Reinbek bei Hamburg: Rowohlt, 1983), 254–66, at 259.
28 Rottmann and Strohm, *Was Sie gegen Mikrozensus und Volkszählung tun können*, 25.
29 Ibid., 7.
30 Several of these articles were published together in the following book: Jochen Bölsche, *Der Weg in den Überwachungsstaat* (Reinbek bei Hamburg: Rowohlt, 1979).
31 Geert Lovink, "From Speculative Media Theory to Net Criticism" (December 19, 1996): www.thing.desk.nl/bilwet/TXT/ICC.txt (accessed October 28, 2017). On the history of the net-criticism movement, see Clemens Apprich, *Vernetzt: Zur Entstehung der Netzwerkgesellschaft* (Bielefeld: Transcript, 2016).
32 Quoted from https://www.fitbit.com/en-ca/whyfitbit.
33 Aly and Roth, *The Nazi Census*, 6.
34 For further discussion of this development, see Turner, *From Counterculture to Cyberculture*, 212–22.
35 George Orwell, *Nineteen Eighty-Four*, The Complete Works of George Orwell, vol. 9 (London: Secker & Warburg, 1987; repr. 1997), 4.
36 Ibid., 3.
37 Ibid., 4.
38 Ibid., 115–16.
39 Ibid., 85.
40 For a literary depiction of this transformation, see Dave Eggers's novel *The Circle* (London: Penguin, 2013).
41 Orwell, *Nineteen Eighty-Four*, 6.
42 Ibid., 214.
43 Ibid.
44 Ibid., 77.
45 Ibid., 82.
46 Ibid., 34.
47 Ibid., 133.
48 Ibid., 174 (emphasis original).
49 Ibid.

50 Ibid., 296.
51 Ibid., 296–7.
52 Ibid., 299.
53 Zygmunt Bauman and David Lyon, *Liquid Surveillance: A Conversation* (Cambridge: Polity, 2013).
54 Finn Brunton and Helen Nissenbaum, *Obfuscation: A User's Guide for Privacy and Protest* (Cambridge, MA: MIT Press, 2015).
55 Quoted from the anonymous article "Tätowierungen," in *Kriminalistik Lexikon*, ed. Waldemar Burghard et al., 2nd edn. (Heidelberg: Kriminalistik-Verlag, 1984), 221.
56 See Kurella, *Cesare Lombroso und die Naturgeschichte des Verbrechers*, 22.
57 Gross, *Criminal Investigation: A Practical Handbook*, 164.
58 Ibid.
59 Ibid., 165.
60 Bertillon, *Das anthropometrische Signalement*, 24.
61 See "Nike's Tattooed Ekins," *New York Times Magazine* (May 22, 1994): www.nytimes.com/1994/05/22/magazine/sunday-may-22-1994-nike-s-tattooed-ekins.html; or Polle de Maagt, "Remarkable Corporate Culture: Nike's Ekin Tattoos," Polledemaagt.com (November 14, 2010): www.polledemaagt.com/blog/2010/11/14/remarkable-corporate-culture-nikes-ekin-tattoos.

5 The Power of Internalization

1 Alfred Ploetz, *Die Tüchtigkeit unsrer Rasse und der Schutz der Schwachen: Ein Versuch über Rassenhygiene und ihr Verhältnis zu den humanen Idealen, besonders zum Socialismus* (Berlin: S. Fischer, 1895), 144.
2 I discussed this development in detail in my book on the history and current practices of artificial reproduction: *Kinder machen. Neue Reproduktionstechnologien und die Ordnung der Familie* (Frankfurt am Main: Fischer Verlag, 2015).
3 Karl Binding and Alfred Hoche, *Allowing the Destruction of Life Unworthy of Life: Its Measure and Form*, trans. Christina Modak (Greenwood, WI: Suzeteo Enterprises, 2012). Originally published as *Die Freigabe der Vernichtung unwerten Lebens: Ihr Mass und ihre Form* (Leipzig: F. Meiner, 1920).
4 Gilles Deleuze, "Postscript on the Societies of Control," *October* 59 (1992), 3–7, at 3–5.
5 Ibid., 7.
6 Quoted from https://www.fitbit.com/en-ca/about.

7 Quoted from https://de-de.facebook.com/pg/generali.giessen/posts/?ref=page_internal.
8 Bauman and Lyon, *Liquid Surveillance*, 32.
9 Georg Lukács, "Reification and the Consciousness of the Proletariat," in *History and Class Consciousness: Studies in Marxist Dialectics*, trans. Rodney Livingstone (Cambridge, MA: MIT Press, 1971), 83–222.
10 This ruling, which concerned a proposed micro-census, was issued in 1969 and is viewable online at the following address: https://www.telemedicus.info/urteile/Allgemeines-Persoenlichkeitsrecht/420-BVerfG-Az-1-BvL-1963-Mikrozensus.html.
11 Oliver Nachtwey, *Die Abstiegsgesellschaft: Über das Aufbegehren in der regressiven Moderne* (Berlin: Suhrkamp, 2016), 108, 11.
12 Ibid., 86.
13 Ibid., 78.
14 Münsterberg, *Grundzüge der Psychotechnik*, 441.
15 Watson, *Behaviorism*, 11. B. F. Skinner similarly stressed the importance of prediction in his standard work *About Behaviorism*, 13–15.
16 See Norbert Wiener et al., "Behavior, Purpose and Teleology," *Philosophy of Science* 10 (1943), 18–24.
17 Herold, "Organisatorische Grundzüge der elektronischen Datenverarbeitung," 254.
18 Michel Foucault, "Subjectivity and Truth," in *About the Beginnings of the Hermeneutics of the Self: Lectures at Dartmouth College, 1980*, trans. Graham Burchell (University of Chicago Press, 2016), 19–52, at 25.
19 Ibid., 25–6.
20 Ulrich Bröckling et al., "Gouvernementalität, Neoliberalismus und Selbsttechnologien: Eine Einleitung," in *Gouvernementalität der Gegenwart: Studien zur Ökonomisierung des Sozialen*, ed. Ulrich Bröckling et al. (Frankfurt am Main: Suhrkamp, 2015), 7–40, at 29.
21 Orwell, *Nineteen Eighty-Four*, 172, 229.
22 The surprising success of the book *Returning to Reims*, in which the sociologist Didier Eribon discusses his lifelong denial of his working-class origins and relates his silence on the matter to the place that "class" occupies in present-day politics, is perhaps an indication that there is renewed interest in this neglected category. See Didier Eribon, *Returning to Reims*, trans. Michael Lucey (Cambridge, MA: MIT Press, 2013).
23 Andreas Reckwitz, *Die Gesellschaft der Singularitäten: Zum Strukturwandel der Moderne* (Berlin: Suhrkamp, 2017), 227

(emphasis original). This book is scheduled to be published in English as *The Society of Singularities* (Cambridge: Polity, 2020).

24 Ibid., 248.

25 If it is characteristic of digital culture that the locus of critique has become problematic in societies composed of networked, self-registering, and self-regulating individuals, then this raises questions about the role of new media technologies in recent political developments. How much of the rise of populism can be attributed to the disposition of a public sphere in which every assertion, every opinion, and every piece of information can be sent to a wide audience without having to pass through the filter of intermediary institutions? Just as Walter Benjamin, in his essay "The Work of Art in the Age of Its Technological Reproducibility," examined the connection between fascism and the new media of film and photography, it would be tempting to analyze the election of Donald Trump and the success of new populist parties in light of today's forms of communication and representation. This, however, would require a full-length study of its own.

Works Cited

Ackermann, Judith. "Location-Based Mobile Gaming in der Stadt: Spielerische Eroberung des urbanen Raums und Hybrid Reality Theatre." In *Mobile Medien – Mobiles Leben: Neue Technologien, Mobilität und die mediatisierte Gesellschaft*. Ed. Thomas Christian Bächle and Caja Thimm. Munster: LIT Verlag, 2014. 143–67.

Aly, Götz. "Die restlose Erfassung im Nationalsozialismus." In *Volkszählungs-Boykott: Bilder, Plakate, Flugschriten*. Kassel, 1987. 12–16.

Aly, Götz, and Karl Heinz Roth. *The Nazi Census: Identification and Control in the Third Reich*. Trans. Assenka Oksiloff. Philadelphia: Temple University Press, 2004.

Anonymous. "Datenschrott für eine Milliarde?" *Der Spiegel* 12 (1987): 30–53.

Apprich, Clemens. *Vernetzt: Zur Entstehung der Netzwerkgesellschaft*. Bielefeld: Transcript, 2016.

Ault, Richard, and James Reese. "A Psychological Assessment of Crime: Profiling." *FBI Law Enforcement Bulletin* 49 (1980): 22–5.

Barlow, John Perry. "A Declaration of the Independence of Cyberspace." Electronic Frontier Foundation (February 8, 1996): https://www.eff.org/cyberspace-independence.

Bartsch, Karl. *Das psychologische Profil und seine Auswertung für Heilpädagogik: Ein Beitrag zur Erforschung der psychischen Funktionen des normalen und abnormalen Kindes*. 2nd edn. Halle an der Saale: C. Marhold, 1926.

Bauman, Zygmunt, and David Lyon. *Liquid Surveillance: A Conversation*. Cambridge: Polity, 2013.

Bélanger, Richard, et al. "U-Shaped Association Between Intensity of Internet Use and Adolescent Health." *Pediatrics* 127 (2011): 330–5.

Benjamin, Walter. "The Work of Art in the Age of Its Technological Reproducibility." Trans. Edmund Jephcott and Harry Zohn. In *The Work of Art in the Age of Its Technological Reproducibility, and Other Writings on Media*. Ed. Michael W. Jennings et al. Cambridge, MA: Harvard University Press, 2008. 19–55.

Bernard, Andreas. *Kinder machen. Neue Reproduktionstechnologien und die Ordnung der Familie*. Frankfurt am Main: Fischer Verlag, 2015.

Bernet, Brigitte. "Der Fall des psychiatrischen Formulars." In *Zum Fall machen, zum Fall werden: Wissensproduktion und Patientenerfahrung in Medizin und Psychiatrie des 19. und 20. Jahrhunderts*. Ed. Sibylle Brändli et al. Frankfurt am Main: Campus, 2009. 62–91.

Bertillon, Alphonse. *Das anthropometrische Signalement: Neue Methode zu Identitäts-Feststellungen. Vortrag am internationalen Congresse für Straf- und Gefängniswesen zu Rom abgehalten*. Berlin: Fischer, 1890.

Bertillon, Alphonse. *La photographie judiciare avec un appendice sur la classification et l'identification anthropométrique*. Paris: Gauthier-Villars, 1890.

Beukers, John. "The Unfolding Future of the Global Navigation Satellite System – Part I: From the Past to the Present." *GPS Solutions* 1 (1995): 23–7.

Binding, Karl, and Alfred Hoche. *Allowing the Destruction of Life Unworthy of Life: Its Measure and Form*. Trans. Christina Modak. Greenwood, WI: Suzeteo Enterprises, 2012.

Bölsche, Jochen. *Der Weg in den Überwachungsstaat*. Reinbek bei Hamburg: Rowohlt, 1979.

Boltanski, Luc. *Mysteries and Conspiracies: Detective Stories, Spy Novels, and the Making of Modern Societies*. Trans. Catherine Porter. Cambridge: Polity, 2014.

Boyd, Danah. "Friendster and Publicly Articulated Social Networks." In *CHI 2004 – Connect: Conference Proceedings*. New York: ACM Press, 2004. N.p.

Boyd, Danah, and Judith Donath. "Public Displays of Connection." *BT Technology Journal* 22 (2004): 71–82.

Boyd, Danah, and Jeffrey Heer. "Profiles as Conversation: Networked Identity Performance on Friendster." In *Proceedings of the 39th Annual Hawaii International Conference on System Sciences*. Los Alamitos: IEEE Computer Society, 2006. N.p.

Brauneisen, Achim. "Die elektronische Überwachung des Aufenthaltsortes als neues Instrument der Führungsaufsicht." *Strafverteidiger* 31 (2011): 311–16.

Bröckling, Ulrich. "Prävention." In *Glossar der Gegenwart*. Ed. Susanne Krasmann et al. Frankfurt am Main: Suhrkamp, 2004. 7–40.

Bröckling, Ulrich. *Das unternehmerische Selbst: Soziologie einer Subjektivierungsform*. Frankfurt am Main: Suhrkamp, 2007.

Bröckling, Ulrich, et al. "Gouvernementalität, Neoliberalismus und Selbsttechnologien: Eine Einleitung." In *Gouvernementalität der Gegenwart: Studien zur Ökonomisierung des Sozialen*. Ed. Ulrich Bröckling et al. Frankfurt am Main: Suhrkamp, 2015. 7–40.

Brunton, Finn, and Helen Nissenbaum. *Obfuscation: A User's Guide for Privacy and Protest*. Cambridge, MA: MIT Press, 2015.

Brussel, James. *The Casebook of a Crime Psychiatrist*. New York: Grove Press, 1968.

Bundesgerichtshof: Überwachung von Personen mittels an Fahrzeugen angebrachter GPS-Empfänger ist grundsätzlich strafbar." *Bundesgerichtshof: Mitteilung der Pressestelle* 96 (2013): http://juris.bundesgerichtshof.de/cgi-bin/rechtsprechung/document.py?Gericht=bgh&Art=pm&Datum=2013&Sort=3&nr=64248&pos=0&anz=95.

Bundestagsdrucksache 17/3403 (2010).

Bundesverfassungsbericht 2 BvR 581/01 (2005).

Burghard, Waldemar, et al., eds. *Kriminalistik Lexikon*. 2nd edn. Heidelberg: Kriminalistik-Verlag, 1984.

Burnett, John, and Alan Bush. "Profiling the Yuppies." *Journal of Advertising Research* 26 (1986): 27–35.

Buschauer, Regine. "(Very) Nervous Systems: Big Mobile Data." In *Big Data: Analysen zum digitalen Wandel von Wissen, Macht und Ökonomie*. Ed. Rámon Reichert. Bielefeld: Transcript, 2014. 405–36.

Buschauer, Regine, and Katharine Willis. *Locative Media: Medialität und Räumlichkeit – Multidisziplinäre Perspectiven zur Verortung der Medien*. Bielefeld: Transcript, 2013.

Crawford, Kate. "When Fitbit Is the Expert Witness." *The Atlantic* (November 19, 2014): https://www.theatlantic.com/technology/archive/2014/11/when-fitbit-is-the-expert-witness/382936.

Crawford, Kate, et al. "Our Metrics, Ourselves: A Hundred Years of Self-Tracking from the Weight Scale to the Wrist Wearable Device." *European Journal of Cultural Studies* 18 (2015): 479–96.

Crawford, Leslie. "Geek Love." *San Francisco Focus* (October, 1996): 20.

Criminal Procedure Code (Strafprozeßordnung, StPO). The Federal Ministry of Justice. September 7, 1998. https://www.google.ca/url?sa=t&rct=j&q=&esrc=s&source=web&cd=5&ved=0ahUKEwi8l-S9g7XWAhXE6oMKHUL0DxsQFgg7MAQ&url=http%3A%2F%2Fwww.track.unodc.org%2FLegalLibrary%2FLegalResources%2FGermany%2FLaws%2FGermany%2520Criminal%2520Procedure%2520Code%25201987(%2520As%2520Amended%25201998).pdf&usg=AFQjCNGxQOQU9Slq65B-86dkSezKG-EBaw.

Cullerre, Alexandre. "Les épileptiques arithmomanes." *Annales médico-psychologiques: Septième série* 11 (1890): 25–36.

Dao, Diep, et al. "Location-Based Services: Technical and Business Issues." *GPS Solutions* 6 (2002): 169–78.

Deleuze, Gilles. "Postscript on the Societies of Control." *October* 59 (1992): 3–7.

Döblin, Alfred. "The Murder of a Buttercup." Trans. Patrick O'Neill. In *Early 20th Century German Fiction*. Ed. Alexander Stephan. New York: Continuum, 2003. 57–67.

Donath, Julius. "Über Arithmomanie." *Zeitschrift für die gesamte Neurologie und Psychiatrie* 43 (1918): 56–64.

Dossier Volkszählung '87. Universität Duisburg Gesamtschule, 1988.

Doyle, Arthur Conan. "The Adventure of the Priory School." In *The Return of Sherlock Holmes*. New York: A. Wessels, 1907. 119–58.

Duve, Freimut. "Katalysator gegen den Orwell-Staat." In *Die Volkszählung*. Ed. Jürgen Taeger. Reinbek bei Hamburg: Rowohlt, 1983. 25–30.

Duytschaever, John. "Eine Pionierleistung des Expressionismus: Alfred Döblins Erzählung 'Die Ermordung einer Butterblume.'" *Amsterdamer Beiträge zur neueren Germanistik* 2 (1973): 27–43.

Eggers, Dave. *The Circle*. London: Penguin, 2013.

Eribon, Didier. *Returning to Reims*. Trans. Michael Lucey. Cambridge, MA: MIT Press, 2013.

Ernst, D. "NAVSTAR/GPS (Global Positioning System) und elektronische Störmaßnahmen." *Ortung und Navigation* 2 (1978): 409–26.

Eylert, Bernd. "Standortbestimmung von Einsatzfahrzeugen." *Die Polizei* 73 (1982): B13–B19.

Feltes, Thomas. "Kriminalität und soziale Kontrolle im 21. Jahrhundert: Eine futuristisches Szenario vor dem Hintergrund aktueller Entwicklungen." *Bewährungshilfe* 35 (1988): 90–102.

Fogy, W. "Positionsbestimmung von Einsatzfahrzeugen im urbanen Gelände." *Ortung und Navigation* 2 (1978): 500–19.

Foucault, Michel. "Subjectivity and Truth." In *About the Beginnings of the Hermeneutics of the Self: Lectures at Dartmouth College, 1980*. Trans. Graham Burchell. University of Chicago Press, 2016. 19–52.

Fox, Richard. "Dr. Schwitzgebel's Machine Revisited: Electronic Monitoring of Offenders." *Australian and New Zealand Journal of Criminology* 20 (1987): 131–47.

Freiesleben, H. C. "Das Satelliten-System NAVSTAR/GPS." *Ortung und Navigation* 2 (1978): 63–79.

Freud, Sigmund. "Further Remarks on the Neuro-Psychoses of Defence." In *The Standard Edition of the Complete Psychological Works of Sigmund Freud, Volume III (1893–1899): Early Psycho-Analytic Publications*. Ed. James Strachey. London: The Hogarth Press, 1962. 157–85.

Freud, Sigmund. "The Neuro-Psychoses of Defence." In *The Standard Edition of the Complete Psychological Works of Sigmund Freud, Volume III (1893–1899): Early Psycho-Analytic Publications*. Ed. James Strachey. London: The Hogarth Press, 1962. 41–61.

Frith, Jordan. *Smartphones as Locative Media*. Cambridge: Polity, 2015.

German Criminal Code. Trans. Michael Bohlander (October 10, 2013): https://www.gesetze-im-internet.de/englisch_stgb/englisch_stgb.html#p0541.

Giese, Fritz. *Psychotechnisches Praktikum*. Halle an der Saale: Wendt & Klauwell, 1923.

Ginzburg, Carlo. "Clues: Roots of an Evidential Paradigm." In *Clues, Myths, and the Historical Method*. Trans. John Tedeschi and Anne C. Tedeschi. Baltimore: Johns Hopkins University Press, 1989. 87–113.

Gold, Louis. "The Psychiatric Profile of the Firesetter." *Journal of Forensic Sciences* 7 (1962): 404–17.

Gould, Stephen Jay. *The Mismeasure of Man*. 2nd edn. New York: W. W. Norton, 1996.

Graaf, Mia de. "'I Was Trying to Find the Right Person to Marry': Match.com Co-Founder Reveals the Inspiration of Online Dating Site as It Goes Public." *Daily Mail* (November 19, 2015): www.dailymail.co.uk/sciencetech/article-3324447/I-trying-right-person-marry-Match-com-founder-reveals-inspiration-online-dating-site-goes-public.html.

Grassegger, Hannes, and Mikael Krogerus. "Ich habe nur gezeigt, dass es die Bombe gibt." *Das Magazin* 48/3 (December 3, 2016): https://www.dasmagazin.ch/2016/12/03/ich-habe-nur-gezeigt-dass-es-die-bombe-gibt.

Griesinger, Wilhelm. "Über einen wenig bekannten psychopathischen Zustand." *Archiv für Psychiatrie und Nervenkrankheiten* 1 (1868): 626–35.

Gross, Hans. *Criminal Investigation: A Practical Handbook*. Trans. John Adam and J. Collyer Adam. Madras: A. Krishnamachari, 1906.

Hall, John. "Electronic Tracking Devices: Following the Fourth Amendment." *FBI Law Enforcement Journal* 54/2 (1985): 26–31.

Hansen, G. R., and W. G. Leflang. *Application of Automatic Vehicle Location in Law Enforcement: An Introductory Planning Guide*. Washington, DC: United States Department of Justice, 1976.

Herold, Horst. "Organisatorische Grundzüge der elektronischen Datenverarbeitung im Bereich der Polizei: Versuch eines Zukunftsmodells." *Taschenbuch für Kriminalisten* 18 (1968): 240–54.

Herold, Horst. "'Rasterfahndung' – Eine computergestützte Fahndungsform der Polizei." *Recht und Politik* 21 (1985): 84–97.

Hess, Volker. "Formalisierte Beobachtung: Die Genese der modernen Krankenakte am Beispiel der Berliner und Pariser Medizin." *Medizinhistorisches Journal* 45 (2010): 293–340.

Hill, Kashmir. "Fitbit Data Just Undermined a Woman's Rape Claim." *Splinter* (June 29, 2015): https://splinternews.com/fitbit-data-just-undermined-a-womans-rape-claim-1793848735.

Hubert, Eva. "Politiker fragen – Bürger antworten nicht! Die Boycottbewegung gegen die Volkszählung." In *Die Volkszählung*. Ed. Jürgen Taeger. Reinbek bei Hamburg: Rowohlt, 1983. 254–66.

Illouz, Eva. *Cold Intimacies: The Making of Emotional Capitalism*. Cambridge: Polity, 2007.

Illouz, Eva. *Why Love Hurts: A Sociological Explanation*. Cambridge: Polity, 2012.

Ipektschi, Ali-Reza. "Ärztliche Aufzeichnungen über Patienten im Allgemeinen Krankenhause in Hamburg in der Zeit von 1823–1888." Doctoral Diss.: Universität Hamburg, 1983.

Jacobson, Len. "GPS: The World's New Utility." *GPS Solutions* 1 (1995): 81.

Jahrreiß, Walter. "Über Zwangsvorstellungen im Verlauf der Schizophrenie." *Archiv für Psychiatrie und Nervenkrankheiten* 77 (1936): 740–88.

Joachim, Georg. *Über Zwangsvorstellungen*. Berlin: Schade, 1892.

Johnson, Carrie. "FBI Still Struggling with Supreme Court's GPS Ruling." National Public Radio (March 21, 2012): www.npr.org/2012/03/21/149011887/fbi-still-struggling-with-supreme-courts-gps-ruling.

Johnston, Rich. "When Spider-Man Invented Electronic Tagging." *Bleeding Cool* (June 24, 2012): https://www.bleedingcool.com/2012/06/24/when-spider-man-invented-electronic-tagging.

Jolin, Annette, and Robert Rogers. "Elektronisch überwachter Hausarrest: Darstellung einer Strafvollzugsalternative in den Vereinigten Staaten." *Monatsschrift für Kriminologie und Strafrechtreform* 73 (1990): 201–9.

Kirkpatrick, David. *The Facebook Effect: The Inside Story of the Company that Is Connecting the World.* New York: Simon & Schuster, 2010.

Kittler, Friedrich. *Gramophone, Film, Typewriter*. Trans. Geoffrey Winthrop-Young and Michael Wutz. Stanford University Press, 1999.

Kob, Janpeter, et al. *Profil der Benutzer öffentlicher Bibliotheken.* Berlin: Deutscher Bibliotheksverband, 1973.

Köhntopp, Kristian, et al. "Ingress – Die Kunst, Umwege zu gehen" (June 22, 2015): http://youarethekey.de/wp-content/uploads/2015/09/Ingress-dieKunstUmwegezugehen.pdf.

Koppenstedt, Franz. "Keine unzumutbaren Fragen bei der Volkszählung." *Frankfurter Allgemeine Zeitung* (April 12, 1983): 7.

Kosinski, Michal, et al. "Our Twitter Profiles, Ourselves: Predicting Personality with Twitter." In *IEEE Third International Conference on Social Computing*. Los Alamitos: IEEE Computer Society, 2011. 180–5.

Kosinski, Michal, et al. "Private Traits and Attributes Are Predictable from Digital Records of Human Behavior." *Proceedings of the National Academy of Sciences* 111 (2013): 5802–5.

Krafft-Ebing, Richard. *Beiträge zur Erkennung und richtigen forensischen Beurtheilung krankhafter Gemütszustände für Aerzte, Richter und Vertheidiger*. Erlangen: Enke, 1867.

Krause, Marcel. "Einleitung Sektion 5: Messen." In *Menschenversuche: Eine Anthologie, 1750–2000*. Ed. Nicolas Pethes et al. Frankfurt am Main: Suhrkamp, 2008. 355–90.

Krüger, [no first name provided]. "Zweckmäßiger Einsatz und Betrieb von Radaranlagen." *Ortung und Navigation* 2 (1978): 105–20.

Kunze, Torsten. "Die electronische Fußfessel in Hessen: Eine positive Betrachtung über Haftvermeidung mit Hilfe zur Selbsthilfe." *Forum Strafvollzug* 57 (2008): 33–5.

Kurella, Hans. *Cesare Lombroso und die Naturgeschichte des Verbrechers*. Hamburg: J. F. Richter, 1892.

Lachapelle, Gerard, and Jinling Wang. "Letter from the Guest Editors: The GPS Wireless Special Issue." *GPS Solutions* 6 (2002): 137.

Larkin, Paul. "The Fourth Amendment and New Technology." *Legal Memorandum* 102 (2013): 1–9.

Lavater, J. C. *Von der Physiognomik*. Leipzig: Weidmann, 1772.

Lavrakis, John W., and Glenn C. Marshall. "Where Is It and Where Is It Going? A Comprehensive Look at GPS Asset Location." *GPS Solutions* 1 (1995): 121–8.

Ledebur, Sophie. "Schreiben und Beschreiben: Zur epistemischen Funktion von psychiatrischen Krankenakten, ihre Archivierung und deren Übersetzung in Fallgeschichten." *Berichte zur Wissenschaftsgeschichte* 34 (2011): 102–24.

Lemke, Thomas. "Test." In *Glossar der Gegenwart*. Ed. Susanne Krasmann et al. Frankfurt am Main: Suhrkamp, 2004. 263–70.

Lichtenberg, Georg Christoph. "Über Physiognomik – Wider die Physiognomen: Zu Beförderung der Menschenliebe und Menschenkenntnis." In *Schriften und Briefe*. Vol. III. Ed. Wolfgang Promies. Munich: Hanser, 1972. 256–95.

Lovink, Geert. "From Speculative Media Theory to Net Criticism" (December 19, 1996): www.thing.desk.nl/bilwet/TXT/ICC.txt.

Löwenfeld, Leopold. *Die psychischen Zwangserscheinungen*. Wiesbaden: J. F. Bergmann, 1904.

Lukács, Georg. "Reification and the Consciousness of the Proletariat." In *History and Class Consciousness: Studies in Marxist Dialectics*. Trans. Rodney Livingstone. Cambridge, MA: MIT Press, 1971. 83–222.

Maagt, Polle de. "Remarkable Corporate Culture: Nike's Ekin Tattoos." Polledemaagt.com (November 14, 2010): www.polledemaagt.com/blog/2010/11/14/remarkable-corporate-culture-nikes-ekin-tattoos.

MacManus, Richard. *Health Trackers: How Technology Is Helping Us Monitor and Improve Our Health*. London: Rowman and Littlefield, 2014.

Marshall, Gary. "The Story of Fitbit: How a Wooden Box Became a $4 Billion Company." *Wearable: Tech for Your Connected Self* (September 9, 2016): https://www.wearable.com/fitbit/youre-fitbit-and-you-know-it-how-a-wooden-box-became-a-dollar-4-billion-company.

Martin-Jung, Helmut. "Verhaltensforschung." *Süddeutsche Zeitung* (May 15, 2007): 1.

Marx, Reiner. "Literatur und Zwangsneurose: Eine Gegenübertragungs-Improvisation zu Alfred Döblins früher Erzählung 'Die Ermordung einer Butterblume.'" In *Internationales Alfred-Döblin-Kolloquium, Leiden 1995*. Ed. Gabrielle Sander. Bern: Peter Lang, 1997. 49–60.

Münsterberg, Hugo. *Grundzüge der Psychotechnik*. 2nd edn. Leipzig: J. A. Barth, 1920.

Münsterberg, Hugo. *On the Witness Stand: Essays on Psychology and Crime*. New York: Clark Boardman, 1923.

Musolff, Cornelia. "Täterprofile und Fallanalyse: Eine Bestandaufnahme." In *Täterprofile bei Gewaltverbrechen: Mythos, Theorie und Praxis des Profilings*. Ed. Cornelia Musolff and Jens Hoffmann. Heidelberg: Springer, 2006. 1–23.

Nachtwey, Oliver. *Die Abstiegsgesellschaft: Über das Aufbegehren in der regressiven Moderne*. Berlin: Suhrkamp, 2016.

Neff, Gina, and Dawn Nafus. *Self-Tracking*. Cambridge, MA: MIT Press, 2016.

Negroponte, Nicholas. *Being Digital*. New York: Knopf, 1995.

Nike's Tattooed Ekins." *New York Times Magazine* (May 22, 1994): www.nytimes.com/1994/05/22/magazine/sunday-may-22-1994-nike-s-tattooed-ekins.html.

Nix, Alexander. "The Power of Big Data and Psychographics in the Electoral Process." Concordia Summit (September 19, 2016): https://www.youtube.com/watch?v=n8Dd5aVXLCc.

Nogala, Detlef, and Rita Haverkamp. "Elektronische Bewachung: Stichworte zur punitiven Aufenthaltskontrolle von Personen." *Datenschutz und Datensicherheit* 24 (2000): 31–8.

Nogala, Detlef, and Fritz Sack. "Folgerungen für die polizeiliche Arbeit aus der Technikausstattung." In *Aktuelle Methoden der Kriminaltechnik und Kriminalistik*. Ed. Heinrich Schielke. Wiesbaden: Bundeskriminalamt, 1995. 115–68.

Olson, Parmy. "Fitbit Now Being Used in the Courtroom." *Forbes* (November 16, 2014): https://www.forbes.com/sites/parmyolson/2014/11/16/fitbit-data-court-room-personal-injury-claim/#1a91f3d27379.

Önel, Günes. "Verfassungsmäßigkeit und Effektivität der 'elektronischen Fußfessel.'" *Jahrbuch des kriminalwissenschaftlichen Institut der Leibniz Universität Hannover* (2012): http://edok01.tib.uni-hannover.de/edoks/e01dh13/76776479Xl.pdf.

Orwell, George. *Nineteen Eighty-Four*. The Complete Works of George Orwell, vol. 9. London: Secker & Warburg, 1987; repr. 1997.

Partridge, Eric, and Henry C. Wyld, eds. *Webster Universal Dictionary: Unabridged International Edition*. New York: Harver, 1968.

Peitz, Konrad. "Bedeutung moderner Ortungs- und Nativigationstechnologien für Gewährleistung der öffentlichen Sicherheit und Ordnung." *Die Polizei* 78 (1987): 361–3.

Penzel, Thomas. "Schlafforschung heute: Entwicklungen, Techniken und Motivationen der Praxis." In *Kontrollgewinn – Kontrollverlust: Die Geschichte des Schlafs in der Moderne*. Ed. Hannah Ahlheim. Frankfurt am Main: Campus, 2014. 209–26.

Piorkowski, Christoph David. "Spurlos im Netz: Wer sich Facebook verweigert, macht sich verdächtig." *Süddeutsche Zeitung* (December 21, 2012): 13.

Ploetz, Alfred. *Die Tüchtigkeit unsrer Rasse und der Schutz der Schwachen: Ein Versuch über Rassenhygiene und ihr Verhältnis zu den humanen Idealen, besonders zum Socialismus*. Berlin: S. Fischer, 1895.

Presidential Decision Directive NSTC-6. March 28, 1996: fas.org/spp/military/docops/national/gps.htm.

Public Urban Locator Service (PULSE): Background and Conference Proceedings. New York: The Institute of Public Administration, 1968.

Püttjer, Christian, and Uwe Schnierda. *Anschreiben und Lebensläufe für Hochschulabsolventen*. Felde am Westensee: Sit-Up Verlag, 1999.

Püttjer, Christian, and Uwe Schnierda. *Das gelungene Online-Bewerbung*. Frankfurt am Main: Campus, 2001.

Püttjer, Christian, and Uwe Schnierda. *Das große Bewerbungshandbuch*. 2nd edn. Frankfurt am Main: Campus, 2006.

Raulff, Ulrich. "Münsterbergs Erfindung oder Der elektrifizierte Zeuge." *Freibeuter* 24 (1985): 33–42.

Rechtschaffen, Allen, and Anthony Kales, eds. *A Manual of Standardized Terminology, Techniques, and Scoring System for Sleep Stages of Human Subjects*. Bethesda: US Department of Health, Education, and Welfare, 1968.

Reckwitz, Andreas. *Die Gesellschaft der Singularitäten: Zum Strukturwandel der Moderne*. Berlin: Suhrkamp, 2017.

Regulation (EU) 2016/679 of the European Parliament and of the Council of 27 April 2016 on the Protection of Natural Persons with Regard to the Processing of Personal Data and on the Free Movement of Such Data, and Repealing Directive 95/46/EC (General Data Protection Regulation)" (2016): http://eur-lex.europa.eu/legal-content/EN/TXT/?uri=CELEX:32016R0679.

Rheingold, Howard. *The Virtual Community: Homesteading on the Electronic Frontier*. 2nd edn. Cambridge, MA: MIT Press, 2000.

Rider, Anthony. "The Firesetter: A Psychological Profile." *FBI Law Enforcement Bulletin* 49 (July 1980): 7–17.

Riordan, Teresa. "Idea for Online Networking Brings Two Entrepreneurs Together." *New York Times* (December 1, 2003): www.nytimes.com/2003/12/01/technology/technology-media-patents-idea-for-online-networking-brings-two-entrepreneurs.html.

Rossolimo, G. I. *Das psychologische Profil und andere experimentell-psychologische, individuale und kollektive Methoden zur Prüfung der Psychomechanik bei Erwachsenen und Kindern*. Halle an der Saale: C. Marhold, 1926.

Rottmann, Verena, and Holger Strohm. *Was Sie gegen Mikrozensus und Volszählung tun können*. Frankfurt am Main: Zweitausendeins, 1987.

Schäffner, Wolfgang. *Die Ordnung des Wahns: Zur Poetologie psychiatrischen Wissens bei Alfred Döblin*. Munich: Fink, 1995.

Schnabel, Christoph. *Datenschutz bei profilbasierten Location Based Services: Die datenschutzadäquate Gestaltung von Service-Plattformen für Mobilkommunikation*. Kassel University Press, 2009.

Schneider, Manfred. *Die erkaltete Herzensschrift: Der autobiographische Text im 20. Jahrhundert*. Munich: C. Hanser, 1986.

Schwartz, Hillel. *Never Satisfied: A Cultural History of Diets, Fantasies, and Fat*. New York: Free Press, 1986.

Schwitzgebel, Ralph K. *Development and Legal Regulation of Coercive Behavior Modification Techniques with Offenders*. Rockville, MD: National Institute of Mental Health, 1971.

Schwitzgebel, Ralph K. "Development of an Electronic Rehabilitation System for Parolees." *Law and Computer Technology* 2/3 (1969): 9–12.

Schwitzgebel, Ralph K., and William Hurd. "Behavioral Supervision System with Wrist Carried Transceiver." United States Patent No. 3478344A (1969): www.google.ch/patents/US3478344.

Schwitzgebel, Ralph K., et al. "A Program of Research in Behavioral Electronics." *Behavioral Science* 9 (1964): 233–8.

Sender, F. "Von TRANSIT zu NAVSTAR: Entwicklungstendenzen der Satellitennavigation." *Ortung und Navigation* 2 (1978): 318–38.

Siegal, Jacob. "One Woman's Fitbit Just Decided a Criminal Case." *BGR* (April 20, 2016): http://bgr.com/2016/04/20/fitbit-fitness-tracker-legal-case.

Skinner, B. F. *About Behaviorism*. New York: Vintage Books, 1974.

Specht, Louis. *Konsequenzen der Ökonomisierung informationeller Selbstbestimmung: Die zivilrechtliche Erfassung des Datenhandels*. Cologne: Heymann, 2012.

Timko, Francis. "Electronic Monitoring – How It All Began: Conversations with Love and Gross." *Journal of Probation and Parole* 17 (1985): 15–16.

Tjardts, Jan Peter. "NAVSTAR GPS: Entwicklungsstand und weitere Zukunft dieses globalen Navigationssystems." *Ortung und Navigation* 6 (1982): 148–58.

Turkle, Sherry. "Constructions and Reconstructions of Self in Virtual Reality: Playing in the MUDS." *Mind, Culture, and Activity* 1 (1994): 158–67.

Turkle, Sherry. *Life on the Screen: Identity in the Age of the Internet*. New York: Simon & Schuster, 1995.

Turner, Fred. *From Counterculture to Cyberculture: Steward Brand, the Whole Earth Network, and the Rise of Digital Utopianism*. University of Chicago Press, 2008.

United States *v.* Jones. 565 U.S. ___, No. 10-1259. 2012.

Using Information from User Video Game Interactions to Target Advertisements." United States Patent No. WO 2007041371 A3 (2007).

Vorpagel, Russel. "Painting Psychological Profiles: Charlatanism, Coincidence, Charisma, Chance, or a New Science?" *The Police Chief* 3 (1982): 156–9.

Watson, John B. *Behaviorism*. New York: Norton, 1925.

Watson, John B. "Psychology as the Behaviorist Views It." *Psychological Review* 20 (1913): 158–77.

Weich, Andreas. "Sich profilieren und profiliert werden: Über zwei Seiten einer Medaille." In *Profile: Interdisziplinäre Beiträge*. Ed. Martin Degeling et al. Lüneburg: Meson Press, 2017. 37–57.

Weinreich, Andrew. "Method and Apparatus for Constructing a Networking Database and System." United States Patent No. US6175831 (1997).

Wenig, Mirko. "TK will Verwendung von Fitnesstrackern im Bonusprogramm belohnen." *Versicherungsbote: Information für Versicherungsmakler* (August 24, 2016): https://www.versicherungsbote.de/id/4844671/Techniker-Krankenkasse-Fitnesstracker-Bonusprogramm.

Wenzlau, Andreas, et al. *KundenProfiling: Die Methode zur Neukundenakquise*. Erlangen: Publicis, 2003.

Wermann, Claus Fokke. "Schöne neue Kabelwelt." In *Volkszählungs-Boykott: Bilder, Plakate, Flugschriten*. Kassel, 1987. 37–9.

Westphal, Carl. "Eigenthümliche mit Einschlafen verbundene Einfälle." In *Carl Westphal's gesammelte Abhandlungen*. Ed. Alexander Westphal. Berlin: Hirschwald, 1892. 393–407.

Wiener, Norbert, et al. "Behavior, Purpose and Teleology." *Philosophy of Science* 10 (1943): 18–24.

Wittig, Petra. "Die datenschutzrechtliche Problematik der Anfertigung von Persönlichkeitsprofilen." *Recht der Datenverarbeitung* 16 (2000): 61–9.

Wolf, Gary. "The Data-Driven Life." *The New York Times Magazine* (April 28, 2010): www.nytimes.com/2010/05/02/magazine/02self-measurement-t.html.

Index